English Literature
for AQA A

D1439619

Tony Childs
Jackie Moore

Heinemann Educational Publishers,
Halley Court, Jordan Hill, Oxford OX2 8EJ
A division of Reed Educational & Professional Publishing Ltd

OXFORD MELBOURNE AUCKLAND
JOHANNESBURG BLANTYRE GABORONE
IBADAN PORTSMOUTH NH (USE) CHICAGO

First published 2000

2004 2003 2002 2001 2000
10 9 8 7 6 5 4 3 2 1

ISBN   0 435 13229 6

Acknowledgements

The Publishers would like to thank the following for permission to use copyright material:

Anvil Press Poetry Ltd for extracts from *Mean Time* by Carol Ann Duffy. Published by Anvil Press Poetry 1993. Reprinted by permission of the publisher; Bloomsbury Publishing for extracts from *Snow Falling on Cedars* by David Guterson. Published by Bloomsbury 1995; David Higham Associates for extracts from *Knowledge of Angels* by Jill Paton Walsh. Published by Black Swan 1994; Faber & Faber Ltd, for extracts from *Arcadia* by Tom Stoppard and extracts from *Whitsun Weddings* by Philip Larkin. Reprinted by permission of the publisher; Peterloo Poets for extracts from *Safe As Houses* by U. A. Fanthorpe. Published by Peterloo Poets, 1982. Copyright © U. A. Fanthorpe. Reprinted by permission of the publisher; Random House for extracts from *Birdsong* by Sebastian Faulks, published by Hutchinson, 1993; *The Bell* by Iris Murdoch, originally published by Chatto & Windus; *The Last Resort* by Alison Lurie, originally published by Chatto & Windus; *The Handmaid's Tale* by Margaret Atwood, originally published by Jonathan Cape; *Enduring Love* by Ian McEwan, originally published by Jonathan Cape. Reprinted by permission of the publisher.

The Publishers have made every effort to trace the copyright holders, but if they have inadvertently overlooked any, they will be pleased to make the necessary arrangements at the first opportunity.

The Publishers would like to thank the following for permission to reproduce photographs: Hulton-Getty p. 127.

Typeset by TechType, Abingdon, Oxon

Printed and bound by Bath Press in the UK

Contents

Introduction

This book is designed to help students following AQA Specification A in Advanced Subsidiary English Literature to work through their course. Its aim is to give you the necessary skills to deal with any of the texts you might study in your course, so that you will feel well prepared and confident when you come to take your exams. You've probably chosen to take English Literature at this level because you enjoyed it at GCSE. This book will help you to build on your GCSE success, and to enjoy the new texts you will be studying at this stage.

This introduction is in two parts:

1 **How this book will help you in your course**
2 **The key to success: Understanding the Assessment Objectives**

How this book will help you in your course

This book is not a guide to individual set texts – after all, texts will change from time to time, and if you take the Shakespeare coursework option the play or plays will be chosen by you and your teachers. Rather, it's a guide to how to approach the texts in order to succeed.

The rest of this introduction will deal with the Assessment Objectives for the specification. It is important that you read through this section carefully before starting on the module. The Assessment Objectives not only underpin all the work in the course, but an understanding of them is also the key to gaining good marks.

The rest of the book deals with each of the three assessment modules for the course. The book will take you through the design and content of each module, with practical advice and exercises. The work you are asked to do will be tailored to the type of assessment involved in the module, which might be external assessment, either open or closed book, or coursework. There will also be examples of the sorts of questions and activities which will be used to test each module as part of the examination.

Finally you will find a Glossary for the book, on pages 171–74.

The key to success: Understanding the Assessment Objectives

Here are the Assessment Objectives for AS English Literature:

The examination will assess a candidate's ability to:
AO1 communicate clearly the knowledge, understanding and insight appropriate to literary study, using appropriate terminology and accurate and coherent written expression
AO2i respond with knowledge and understanding to literary texts of different types and periods
AO3 show detailed understanding of the ways in which writers' choices of form, structure and language shape meanings
AO4 articulate independent opinions and judgements, informed by different interpretations of literary texts by other readers
AO5i show understanding of the contexts in which literary texts are written and understood

As you can see, the Assessment Objectives define the literary skills which you have to show in the course. It is vital to understand that they have different numbers of marks in different modules. For example, in Module 3, which is the Pre and Post 1900 Drama and Poetry module, the 30 marks available are divided like this:

AO1 5 marks
AO2i 5 marks
AO3 5 marks
AO4 10 marks
AO5i 15 marks.

In this module, you have to choose a twentieth-century text and a pre-twentieth-century text. On the pre-twentieth-century text, you will be assessed on AO5i, but not on AO4. For the twentieth-century text, it's the other way round – AO4 (interpretations), and not AO5i (contexts).

So the marks depend on the Assessment Objectives, and the marks vary in the different modules, and sometimes in the different sections too. That's why there are boxes at the beginning of each of the three modules to show you exactly which Assessment Objectives count in that module and how many marks each one carries.

What the Assessment Objectives mean

Assessment Objective 1

> AO1 communicate clearly the knowledge, understanding and insight
> appropriate to literary study, using appropriate terminology and accurate
> and coherent written expression

This means that you have to be able to do three things:

- Construct clear and logical arguments. This is an important part of
  communicating *clearly* and being *coherent*. It means that whatever task you
  undertake in the course, it's important to sequence your response effectively
  – which means planning it carefully.

- Acquire appropriate literary terminology, so that you can express your
  opinions about literary texts precisely and clearly. There will be a lot of terms
  you already know, but you'll come across more during the course, which you
  need to understand to use effectively in your writing. The Glossary at the end
  of the book might be useful for you to refer to, although it doesn't include
  every literary term you might come across.

- Make sure that what you write is legible, and that spelling, grammar and
  punctuation are accurate, so that your meaning is clear.

This Assessment Objective is tested in every module, so it's very important.

Assessment Objective 2i

> AO2i respond with knowledge and understanding to literary texts of different
> types and periods

There are three things to think about here.

First, you have to show knowledge. AO1 includes the way you communicate that
knowledge and develop your argument but that is only valid if it's supported by
evidence from the text. Details from the text you're writing about, quotations
from it, echoes of it, would all demonstrate your knowledge. With texts that
you're studying for exams (which is all of them unless you're choosing the
coursework option on the Shakespeare module), you'll need to be very familiar
with them when you go into the exam. For Modules 2 and 3 you *can* take the
texts into the exam with you, but just to look at passages which might be
referred to in exam questions. You will still need to be as familiar with the texts
as you are for those in Module 1, which you can't take into the exam.

Understanding has to be shown too. This will be revealed by the way you write about the ideas in the text – your understanding of the writer's ideas and concerns, and your own ideas about them.

'Different types and periods' is covered by the specifications for AS Level which must meet these requirements:

- at least four texts must be studied

- prose must be studied

- drama must be studied

- a play by Shakespeare must be studied

- one text other than Shakespeare, published before 1900, must be studied.

The texts you have to choose from in Modules 1, 2 and 3 meet this part of the objective.

Assessment Objective 3

> AO3 detailed understanding of the ways in which writers' choices of form, structure and language shape meanings

This Assessment Objective deals with how the writers of the texts work. What methods do they use to enable them to express their ideas and meanings? How effective are the methods they have chosen? Here's a breakdown of what this Assessment Objective means in detail.

Meanings

The important thing in this Assessment Objective is the relationship between means and purposes – not just the methods the writers choose to use, but why they use them, the effects they're trying to create in the reader's mind and why. It's worth noticing, though, that the word 'meanings' in the Assessment Objective is plural. A particular use of form, or structure, or language might create several possible meanings, not just one.

Writers' choices

In the questions which test this objective, it's important to keep the writer at the centre of your discussion. The writer of any piece of literature makes choices all the time about which words to use, in what order, and so on. You do this yourself, with anything you write. You need to be aware, for example, if you are studying poetry, of the verse form the writer is using, the patterns and the characteristics of the language and why the writer has made these choices.

Form

In each of the three genres defined by the specification, writers will have made choices of form. Here are some examples of the sort of things you might be thinking about.

In prose, the writer's first decision was probably whether to write a novel or a short story. The writer might have chosen to write in the first person or the third, or a mixture, and might have used different types of prose within the text, such as diaries or letters. The book might fall into a recognisable genre, an allegory or a horror story, and therefore the form chosen is likely to be the standard form for this type of novel. The book might be divided into chapters, or it might be continuous prose; there might be an epilogue. You need consider the effect of these choices and why the writer made them.

A poet may have chosen to write in verses or stanzas. There might be a strict rhyme scheme, perhaps in a traditional form such as a sonnet, or blank verse, or free verse. There might be a definite rhythm, which is repeated throughout the poem, or it might vary. You need to consider why the poet might have chosen to vary the rhythm and the effect it has.

With drama, you might be looking at verse drama, or prose dialogue. Shakespeare, for instance, wrote his plays mostly in verse, but used prose as well, and you can consider why he chose to have particular passages in prose rather than verse. Is the play you're looking at divided into Acts and Scenes. What effect does this have?

Structure

The novel or story being studied might be written chronologically or might employ time shifts, such as flashbacks. If these occur in a systematic way, you can consider what patterns are there and the effect they have on the reader. It may be important to the novelist to reveal things at a certain point, or to set certain events or ideas against each other. Some other structural questions might be: are the chapters organised in a particular way? Do they begin or end in a way which forms a pattern? Are there passages or chapters which don't advance the plot but give information vital for the reader? Do they form a pattern?

Structure, as we've seen, is about beginnings, middles and ends – the sequence of things, why they're in the order they're in, and so on. In poetry, the structure might be shown through the way the verses or stanzas are presented – there might be a logical progression of thought, for instance, with each verse or stanza moving the thought on, or offering a different perspective on the subject of the poem. How does the poem end? With a concluding thought, a universal thought, a change of mood? How has the poem prepared the reader for this ending? When you've read several poems by the same poet, as you will in Module 3, you might start to see uses of structures which are characteristic of the poet.

Some of the ideas about the structure of prose and poetry apply to drama, too – why Acts and Scenes begin and end in the way they do, and why they're ordered in the way they are. For instance, in *Antony and Cleopatra* the early scenes alternate between Rome and Egypt. Shakespeare has clearly made this choice so that the audience starts to compare the qualities of the two places, and the differences between them. The audience could be offered another angle on one of the dramatist's ideas in a sub-plot – for instance, the Gloucester plot in *King Lear* forms a parallel story about family relationships and blindness. This is a structural device.

Language

First- and third-person narratives are defined by language – the use of 'I' and 'my', for instance. If the author's voice appears in the text, how is this presented through language? In the same way, writers may choose to vary tense for a particular effect – a sudden switch from past to present to produce a feeling of immediacy is an obvious example.

All sorts of patterns of words and imagery might appear in a novel. 'Poetic' language isn't just used in poetry, of course – imagery, for instance, can be used effectively in prose and drama. It is likely that there will be more language devices concentrated together in poetry, though. When people refer to 'poetic' prose, this is what they mean – there are a lot of devices, and the language is heightened. Of course, the reverse can also be true – a poet might choose to use very plain, simple language in a poem, or in part of a poem, to create a particular effect.

There are a number of devices which you find most often in poetry. You need to know the terms for them, and what they mean, to meet Assessment Objective 1, but for Assessment Objective 3 you need to be able to write about how they work, and why poets choose to use them. Just as in prose, it's patterns of language use you need to look for, too, either in a particular poem or in a poet's work.

In some ways the study of the language of drama is no different to that of poetry and prose – you need to consider whether plain language or heightened language is used, formal or informal register, and so on, and the writer's reasons for these choices. Drama is written to be performed, though, rather than read, so the audience hear the words once. In order to create realistic characters on stage, the playwright will choose language which creates particular and individual characters. The language may try to capture the words and rhythms of ordinary daily speech too, according to the content or setting of the play.

Example of this Assessment Objective 'in action'

For Assessment Objective 3 it's important to consider how these elements might work together, and that you're looking at them to see how they 'shape meanings'.

Here's an example of form, structure and language working together to express meanings, from *Hamlet*, Act 4 Scene 7.

> QUEEN GERTRUDE   There is a willow grows aslant a brook,
> That shows his hoar leaves in the glassy stream;
> There with fantastic garlands did she come,
> Of crow-flowers, nettles, daisies, and long purples,
> That liberal shepherds give a grosser name,
> But our cold maids do dead men's fingers call them:
> There, on the pendent boughs her coronet weeds
> Clambering to hang, an envious sliver broke,
> When down her weedy trophies and herself
> Fell in the weeping brook. Her clothes spread wide,
> And, mermaid-like, awhile they bore her up;
> Which time she chanted snatches of old tunes,
> As one incapable of her own distress,
> Or like a creature native and indu'd
> Unto that element; but long it could not be
> Till that her garments, heavy with their drink,
> Pull'd the poor wretch from her melodious lay
> To muddy death.
>
> LAERTES   Alas! then, she is drown'd?
> QUEEN GERTRUDE   Drown'd, drown'd.
> LAERTES   Too much of water hast thou, poor Ophelia,
> And therefore I forbid my tears; . . .

In this passage, Gertrude is describing the death of Ophelia. Shakespeare has made a series of interesting choices of form, language and structure here for the audience to interpret. The language is lyrical, heightened with words such as 'pendent' and 'coronet', and the brook personified as 'weeping', adding to the elegiac, grief-stricken tone. It's also full of sexual allusions, particularly in the choices of the flowers, such as the 'long purples'. Interestingly, this is not at all typical of Gertrude in the play. Although her sexual behaviour is at the heart of the problem, she hasn't spoken in such a suggestive way before, and her speech has been straightforward, not like this at all. This change in the pattern of her language may suggest that the writer is shaping some particular meanings here.

The interesting feature of form comes at the end of her speech. Laertes asks, 'Alas! then, she is drown'd?', which seems a pretty obvious conclusion; but it allows Gertrude to repeat, 'Drown'd, drown'd', the repetition in itself creating an emotional underscoring. The line is incomplete, however; both syllables have to be stressed, which is arresting in itself, and then there's a gap of eight syllables before the next line. What happens in this gap? The audience is looking, presumably, at the silent, sorrowing Queen.

This can be seen as a key moment in the structure of the play. The positioning of Gertrude's speech here helps to cancel out the memory of her earlier lasciviousness and betrayal, of her son as well as her first husband, and her unfeeling behaviour towards both of them, so that when she dies at the end of the play a range of responses may be elicited from the audience. Her death accentuates the treachery of Claudius and the sense of Hamlet's loss. The tragedy of her own death (which we are much more likely to view as tragic after the Ophelia death speech) is an important factor in the whole tragic effect of the play's ending. Shakespeare has used form, language and structure together to shape meaning, and to influence the audience's response.

Assessment Objective 4

AO4   articulate independent opinions and judgements, informed by different interpretations of literary texts by other readers

There are a number of things to consider here, which affect the way you need to think about your texts, and, of course, how you'll be tested on them. There are two parts to this objective. The first part – '*articulate independent opinions and judgements*' – is the only part tested in Modules 1 and 2. In Module 3, where it is the dominant Assessment Objective, the whole objective is tested. Here's a breakdown of what it means in detail.

- **'articulate independent opinions and judgements'**

Texts have different meanings for different readers – there's no single meaning which is the 'right' one. In the exam candidates will be expected to take part in genuine critical enquiry – and this means that the teachers and examiners who assess your responses will not work to a 'right' answer which they've got and you haven't. It's your overview and judgement, and the way you go about it, which will be assessed. Therefore you need to be confident enough in your knowledge and understanding of the text to be able to form a clear personal and independent judgement about what it means to you.

- **'informed by different interpretations of literary texts by other readers'**

The central premise here is that there is no single interpretation of any literary text. Readers of texts are all different, because everybody is affected by their own experiences and background. The way we interpret texts and their meanings can depend on who we are, and the way we've come to the reading of the text.

In the same way, literary texts may be understood differently in different historical periods, and by different social groups. Texts are bound to embody the attitudes and values of their writers, who in turn may represent the attitudes and values of a particular society or social group. Texts do not, therefore, reflect an external, objective reality. Reality means different things for different people at different times. In a way, all books are rewritten and reinterpreted by the societies which read them.

Assessment Objective 5i

> AO5i understanding of the contexts in which literary texts are written and understood.

At AS level, this objective is only tested in Module 3, on the pre-twentieth-century texts, but it is still important to understand what it means. There are many contextual frames surrounding literary texts – that is to say, many facts and processes which have shaped the way they were written.

Here are some of the important types of relevant context:

- The context of a period or era, including significant social, historical, political and cultural processes. This applies to the period in which a text is set, or the period in which it was written, which may not be the same thing.

- The context of the work in terms of the writer's biography and/or milieu.

- The context of the work in terms of other texts, including other works by the same author. So, it might be interesting to look at the alternative ways Shakespeare's concerns are presented in different plays.

- The different contexts for a work established by its reception over time, including the recognition that works have different meanings and effects upon readers in different historical periods.

- The content of a given or specific passage in terms of the whole work from which it is taken, a part-to-whole context. So, you could look at a scene in a play in terms of the play's structure, mood and language, for example.

- The literary context, including the question of generic factors and period-specific styles. For instance, when looking at a Restoration comedy you would want to consider the stage and comedy conventions of the Restoration, and how the text conforms to them.

- The language context, including relevant and significant episodes in the use and development of literary language. This might include matters of style, such as the use of **colloquial**, **dialect** or **demotic** language.

Module ① The Modern Novel

This module carries 30% of the total marks for the AS course. The marks are divided amongst the Assessment Objectives like this:

──── ASSESSMENT OBJECTIVES ────

AO1 communicate clearly the knowledge, understanding and insight appropriate to literary study, using appropriate terminology and accurate and coherent written expresssion
(7% of the final AS mark; 3.5% of the final A level mark)

AO2i respond with knowledge and understanding to literary texts of different types and periods
(10% of the final AS mark; 5% of the final A level mark)

AO3 show detailed understanding of the ways in which writers' choices of form, structure and language shape meanings
(8% of the final AS mark; 4% of the final A level mark)

AO4 articulate independent opinions and judgements (the first part of this Assessment Objective).
(5% of the final AS mark; 2.5% of the final A level mark)

Content

This module meets the prose requirement for the syllabus and requires the detailed study of one modern novel.

Understanding your text

From a very young age, children start to gain knowledge of stories. Take, for example, the tale of the Three Little Pigs. There were three houses made of straw, wood and brick, and a wolf who huffed and puffed and blew the first two down. However, it was probably not until you were older that you would have thought about the meaning of the story and realised that it was a moral tale about the virtues of prudence, caution and wisdom.

That's the difference between knowing and understanding; you knew the plot first, and then learned to understand themes later. The word 'theme' is generally used to indicate the purposes or concerns of the writer; the deeper ideas which lie behind the plot.

ACTIVITY 1

In groups, remind yourselves of the tale of Little Red Riding Hood. First of all, work through the story, and then discuss the ideas or themes behind the plot.

As you do so, you should be asking yourself two questions:

1 What ideas are being conveyed to the readers?

2 What lessons may be learned from this tale?

ACTIVITY 2

Now remind yourself of a novel you read for GCSE. Under two headings 'Plot' and 'Themes', fill in details about this novel.

Understanding the difference between plot and themes is the first stage in achieving the knowledge and understanding referred to in the second Assessment Objective.

Here is an extract from Iris Murdoch's novel *The Bell*. Four of the residents of Imber Court are watching Peter Topglass ring some of the wild birds he has trapped so that they may be traced in the future:

> Then with his left hand he bent the flexible band around the bird's leg, and lifting it up to his mouth closed the band deftly with his teeth. At the sight of Peter's strong teeth closing so near to that tiny twig of a leg, Dora could bear it no longer and turned away . . . Dora was full of wonderment and distress and Paul was laughing at her. Michael looked at Toby. His eyes were wide and his lips moist and red where he had been biting them. Michael now laughed at Toby. It was extraordinary how affecting the whole business was.

These are some of the things going on in the story or plot:

- Peter Topglass is a student of bird life, an ornithologist.

- There is some description of birds being ringed for tracing later.

- He is watched as he does this by four other members of the community.

- They each show different reactions to this process.

But there are also a number of other underlying ideas and themes which emerge from the passage:

- Iris Murdoch has used this incident to show the different responses by the various characters. These in turn suggest characteristics which will become important later in the book.

- Peter is seen to be professional and precise.

- Dora is shown to be sensitive and compassionate.

- Paul is rather heartless as he laughs.

- Toby is wide-eyed and rather inexperienced.

- Michael is calmer. He is concerned with Toby, and you see Toby through Michael's eyes, with his 'moist and red' lips. Why do you think this is?

- The central image in this extract is the entrapment and ringing of innocent creatures for further knowledge. At the same time it is being suggested that the actual characters themselves are 'entrapped' in Imber Court. They become 'ringed' as you see what they learn about themselves and others during the course of the novel.

If you put these two sets of ideas together you have both knowledge and understanding of the extract.

The following extract is from Margaret Atwood's novel, *The Handmaid's Tale*. The narrator, Offred, is a handmaid. Her job is to produce children for a Commander and his wife who cannot have any of their own. In this extract she watches one of the other handmaids give birth:

> To the left, the double doors to the dining room are folded back, and inside I can see the long table, covered with a white cloth and spread with a buffet: ham, cheese, oranges – they have oranges! – and fresh-baked breads and cakes. As for us, we'll get milk and sandwiches, on a tray, later. But they have a coffee urn, and bottles of wine, for why shouldn't the Wives get a little drunk on such a triumphant day? First they'll wait for the results, then they'll pig out. They're gathered in the sitting room on the other side of the stairway now, cheering on this Commander's Wife, the Wife of Warren. A small thin woman, she lies on the floor, in a white cotton nightgown, her greying hair spreading like mildew over the rug; they massage her tiny belly, just as if she's really about to give birth herself.

ACTIVITY 3

Read this extract, and then analyse it using the checklist below:

1 First identify what is happening in the plot or storyline.

2 Then work out the ideas behind the extract. You may consider, for example:

- what you learn about the role of handmaids

- what you learn of their status in society

- what you learn about the attitudes and behaviour of the wives.

In this way, you are achieving *'knowledge and understanding'* of the writer's ideas, which is the first part of the second Assessment Objective. This knowledge and understanding also needs to demonstrate consideration of the ways in which writers present their ideas. This is the third Assessment Objective, to *'show detailed understanding of the ways in which writers' choices of form, structure and language shape meanings'*.

How writers shape meanings

One of the differences between prose and poetry lies in the language used, as prose writers often use 'everyday' language. The use of language, however, can be very similar in poetry and prose.

Writers of prose, like writers of poetry, use **figurative language** to bring words to life, to give them emphasis and impact, and to give them an extended range of meaning, as you will see in the next section.

Exploring the language of prose

In Alice Walker's novel, *The Color Purple*, the American female narrator has had a rotten childhood and an equally rotten marriage. However, she has made a friendship with another woman who has taught her that there is beauty and love in life:

> Naw, she say. God made it. Listen, God love everything you love – and a mess of stuff you don't. But more than anything else, God love admiration.
>
> You saying God vain? I ast.
>
> Naw, she say. Not vain, just wanting to share a good thing. I think it pisses God off if you walk by the color purple in a field somewhere and don't notice it.

In this extract, the colour purple is used to indicate God's love, admiration and wonder. But the word 'purple' may also have other significances, such as:

• death and mourning

• the robes of royalty

• other significances personal to you.

So you have seen that the word 'purple' has gathered up many meanings. When these various meanings are generally agreed they are called **connotations** but, when they are personal to the reader they are called **associations**.

ACTIVITY 4

Choose another colour such as red, black, white or gold, and list the different connotations and associations which occur to you.

Many words have different connotations. Take, for example, the word 'woods'. Here is an extract from a poem called 'Stopping by Woods on a Snowy Evening' by Robert Frost:

The woods are lovely, dark, and deep,
But I have promises to keep,
And miles to go before I sleep, . . .

What does the word 'woods' suggest? Could it be leisure time? Something that is secret and exciting? Or could it be death and peace?

The accumulation of a number of meanings around words also occurs in prose writing. In the next extract, from the novel *Cold Mountain* by Charles Frazier, a young soldier tries to find his way home after running away from the battlegrounds of the American Civil War:

He sat awhile on a rock, and then got up and walked all morning through the dim woods. The track was ill used, so coiled and knotted he could not say what its general tendency was. It aimed nowhere certain but up. The brush and bracken grew thick in the footway, and the ground seemed to be healing over, so that in some near future the way would not even remain as scar . . . Only the black trunks were visible, rising into the low sky like old menhirs stood up by a forgotten race to memorialize the darkest events of their history.

*menhirs are tall, upright stones which are monuments, such as Stonehenge.

ACTIVITY 5

What do you think the woods are used to suggest here? You should think about:

• the use of the words 'dim' and 'ill used'

• the references to being lost

• the references to 'scar' and 'healing'

• the reference to the 'darkest events of their history'.

How do these words tell you something about the experiences and the state of mind of the soldier?

The word 'woods' might also have other associations from your childhood memories or your own reading, for example:

- Little Red Riding Hood met the wolf in the woods
- Hansel and Gretel nearly died in the woods
- Shakespeare uses woods to suggest areas of magic, dreams, love and secrecy in *A Midsummer Night's Dream*.

ACTIVITY 6

Choose a couple of words such as 'sea', 'snow', 'fire' or 'water'. Write down the **connotations** and **associations** which these words hold for you. Then compare these with a partner.

As well as carefully choosing individual words, prose writers, like poets, use **imagery** to draw attention to what they are writing about, and to try to make the reader see things in a new light. The use of imagery allows links or comparisons to be made between one idea and another and to achieve particular effects. Sometimes the link is obvious, but sometimes it can be unexpected or even shocking. In this way ideas can be conveyed powerfully and with impact, making the reader use his or her imagination and experience to understand what the writer is trying to say. Two types of figurative language are **similes** and **metaphors**.

Similes

Think about how you might describe a child or a friend. You might use phrases like:

- 'She is as pretty as a picture'; or
- 'He is as sweet as sugar'; or of a boxer, for example,
- 'He fought like a lion'.

All of these examples use a **simile**, a comparison of two things linked by the words 'as' or 'like'.

How do these comparisons work?

- 'She is as pretty as a picture' calls up a visual image. She is compared to a beautiful painting, so the image reinforces the idea of perfection. That is the point of this simile.
- 'He is as sweet as sugar' is a simile which suggests taste, the sweetness of sugar; the boy is sweet, but sugar can also be too sweet. The phrase therefore suggests that the sweetness could be a little too much.

- 'He fought like a lion' suggests qualities that we associate with lions, such as strength, power, danger, wildness, courage, fear. There is also an association with touch here, implied in the thought of those dreadful claws tearing at somebody or something.

ACTIVITY 7

Write six sentences using similes with the words 'as' and 'like'. Try to include the different senses of taste, touch, sight, sound and smell. Following the model above, try to explain the effects of the similes.

How do similes work in literary prose texts?

Here are two examples from Jill Paton Walsh's novel, *Knowledge of Angels*. Part of the main plot of the novel is the attempt by a monk called Beneditx to persuade a stranger, Palinor, to believe in God by using reason.

In this novel the writer uses similes sparingly, but when they do appear they often have associations with events that occur later in the novel.

In the first example, the writer describes the view of the countryside as Palinor first rides through it.

They were approaching Ciudad, and little towers topped by a ring of sails like the petals of a sunflower were scattered everywhere, spinning in the evening air.

ACTIVITY 8

Look at the simile used here: 'like the petals of a sunflower'. What effect does this simile have on you? You might think about:

- why the sails are compared to flowers

- what this tells you about the look and atmosphere of the place.

A second example is the writer's use of a simile to describe reason:

. . . Beneditx had said that reason, even at the height of its powers, was like the mounting block at the monastery gate – it served to give a leg up to faith.

---

*A *mounting block* is made of stone. It is high enough to enable a rider to mount the horse.

ACTIVITY 9

In this example, the writer explains her own use of the simile. How do you think the simile works in its comparison of reason to a mounting block?

Later in the novel, Jill Paton Walsh returns to this image. She develops it when Beneditx admits he is confused by Palinor's replies to his arguments:

> I was founded on reason. And now the mounting block is kicked away from under me, and without it I cannot mount and ride. I have no strength to gain the saddle of the fine steed that bore me once so proudly!

ACTIVITY 10

1 How does this simile now extend the meaning of the first simile?

2 What does it suggest about the state of mind of Beneditx?

The similes make us question how the author wants us to think about things. These questions and ideas help us to create many meanings, and to gather meanings as we read through the book. This is called a **cumulative process**.

Metaphors

A metaphor works like an abbreviated simile, without the words 'as' or 'like'. It is a comparison in which one thing is given the qualities of another. For example, you might say 'He stretched himself to the limit in his studies', knowing that he did not *literally* stretch himself. The image likens him to a piece of elastic, to suggest how hard the boy worked or 'stretched' himself. As in poetry, the use of metaphor is important to writers of prose texts.

You probably use metaphors in your everyday speech without realising it. If you were to describe someone as a 'wet blanket' you would not mean that literally. You would mean that the person had 'dampened' your enthusiasm just as a blanket might be used to put out a fire.

ACTIVITY 11

Now make a list of six metaphors that you use in everyday speech.

Writers use metaphors to create layers of meaning in their writing. In her novel *Knowledge of Angels*, Jill Paton Walsh uses a central metaphor throughout the book. She compares Beneditx's attempts to persuade Palinor that God exists to a game of chess:

He [Palinor] awaited Beneditx with the kind of interest a chess player takes in the prospect of a worthy opponent.

The difference between a real game of chess and the metaphorical game in the novel is that if Palinor wins the game he will lose his life.

At the centre of his novel *Enduring Love*, the novelist Ian McEwan uses the metaphor of a balloon going up. At the beginning of the novel, the narrator Joe and his girlfriend Clarissa watch as the flight goes out of control, and the men try to hold the balloon down:

. . . someone let go, and the balloon and its hangers-on lurched upwards another several feet . . . But letting go was in our nature too. Selfishness is also written on our hearts . . . By the time I got to my feet the balloon was fifty yards away, and one man was still dangling by his rope.

ACTIVITY 12

Study this episode to see how the writer develops ideas about human nature, and ask yourself these questions:

- How much control do we really have in our lives?

- What is our responsibility to others?

In the next extract from *The Bonfire of the Vanities*, a novel by Tom Wolfe, the writer criticises the greed, materialism and consumerism of twentieth-century American life. The central character, Sherman McCoy, has just arrived at a society party and is surveying the women he sees there.

The women came in two varieties. First, there were women in their late thirties and in their forties and older (women 'of a certain age'), all of them skin and bones (starved to near perfection) . . . They were the social X-rays, to use the phrase that had bubbled up into Sherman's own brain. Second, there were the so-called Lemon Tarts. These were women in their twenties or early thirties, mostly blondes (the Lemon in the Tarts), who were the second, third, or fourth wives or live-in girlfriends of men over forty or fifty or sixty (or seventy), the sort of women men refer to, quite without thinking, as *girls* . . . What was entirely missing from *chez* Bavardage was that manner of woman who is neither very young nor very old, who has laid in a lining of subcutaneous fat, who glows with plumpness and a rosy face that speaks, without a word, of home and earth . . . and conversations while seated on the edge of the bed, just before the Sandman comes. In short, no one ever invited . . . Mother.

This single paragraph makes a cutting attack on the nature of society life in modern New York. The effect rests on a sequence of seven metaphors, but Tom Wolfe uses these metaphors in a very clever way by using two contrasted sets of images. He uses the first two metaphors to ridicule what he sees in this society:

1 The 'social X-rays': these are the fashionable anorexic socialites. The force of the metaphor comes from the fact that these women are so thin you could see through them as if they were X-ray films.

2 The 'Lemon Tarts': these are the typical hangers-on who attach themselves to the rich men whom he sees in his society. The image is multi-faceted, as the lemon could be the dyed blonde hair, the tart, the loose morality of the woman. Also, like actual lemon tarts, these women are to be devoured by the men, or perhaps by their own social ambitions.

The first two metaphors, therefore, describe the women whom McCoy sees as he looks around the room. The writer then goes on to explain what is missing in this society in the next sequence of metaphors.

ACTIVITY 13

Discuss in groups the significance of the next sequence of four metaphors:

1 the woman who 'who has laid in a lining of subcutaneous fat'

2 she 'glows with plumpness and a rosy face'

3 she 'speaks, without a word, of home and earth'

4 ' . . . before the Sandman comes'.

The last sentence is also very telling: 'In short, no one ever invited . . . Mother.'

Discuss the ways in which Wolfe has used the word 'Mother' to pull together the ideas in this extract.

Tom Wolfe has used metaphor here as a type of shorthand to attack his society with very few words.

There are two other style issues to look at in this extract:

Word-order: writers generally order their words carefully. Important words usually occur at the beginnings and ends of sentences. Here the key word 'Mother' is held until the very last word of the paragraph.

Pacing: note how Tom Wolfe has paced the important last line of this extract: he has put in three dots to make a deliberate pause before the important last word. This has the effect of making the reader wonder briefly what to expect and gives the final word more impact.

The whole paragraph is carefully controlled through choice of language, word-order and pacing.

Now read this extract from the novel *One Flew Over the Cuckoo's Nest* by Ken Kesey. The novel is about inmates in an asylum, which Kesey calls the Combine. He sarcastically presents the hospital as a mending factory for society, run by Big Nurse. The narrator himself is an inmate.

> Yes. This is what I know. The ward is a factory for the Combine. It's for fixing up mistakes made in the neighbourhoods and in the schools and in the churches, the hospital is. When a completed product goes back out into society, all fixed up good as new, *better* than new sometimes, it brings joy to the Big Nurse's heart: something that came in all twisted different now is a functioning, adjusted component, a credit to the whole outfit and a marvel to behold. Watch him sliding across the land with a welded grin, fitting into some nice little neighbourhood where they're just now digging trenches along the street to lay pipes for city water. He's happy with it. He's adjusted to surroundings finally . . .

Kesey uses a specific **register** to describe the hospital and its inmates. He presents the hospital as a factory called the Combine, which works for society. Patients come in to be 'repaired', to be made suitable to fill an allotted role in society.

ACTIVITY 14

Working alone or in groups, analyse the sequence of metaphors, and then explore how effective they are in achieving what you think the author's purposes are.

These extracts and activities have shown that there are many similarities between the language of prose and the language of poetry. You will need to scrutinise the language of a novel as closely as you will look at the language of the poetry you study when you move on to Modules 2 and 3.

You will also be building up a critical vocabulary, which will help you to gain marks by using the 'appropriate terminology' mentioned in the first Assessment Objective. So far you have considered connotation, association, cumulative effect, similes, metaphors, word-order and pacing. But remember: these terms are only meaningful when used to explain how writers achieve their meaning. Using critical terms without providing evidence from the text has no value. Always try to explain how figures of speech are used to achieve particular effects.

Varieties of prose writing

There are other ways in which language is used more specifically in the writing of novels and short stories. The following sections will cover varieties of prose writing, and structure and structural devices in order to complete work on the third Assessment Objective.

Narrative prose

All the prose you will read for this module is narrative prose, in that it narrates or tells a story. Within narrative prose there are several types of prose writing, and you may well find that your own text includes several types.

Here is the beginning of a novel, *Enduring Love*, by Ian McEwan:

> The beginning is simple to mark. We were in sunlight under a turkey oak, partly protected from a strong, gusty wind. I was kneeling on the grass with a corkscrew in my hand, and Clarissa was passing me the bottle – a 1987 Daumas Gassac. This was the moment, this was pinprick on the time map: I was stretching out my hand, and as the cool neck and the black foil touched my palm, we heard a man's shout. We turned to look across the field and saw the danger. Next thing, I was running towards it. The transformation was absolute . . .

On a first reading, it seems that just a few facts are given in this opening paragraph:

- the narrator, Joe, and his girlfriend, Clarissa, are having a picnic

- it is a very windy day

- as he is about to open the wine, they see something happening, something which is evidently dangerous.

On a second reading, however, you realise that there are other things going on, which raise a few questions:

- What exactly is it the beginning of?

- Why might the author stress that it is windy?

- What could the writer mean by his reference to the 'pinprick on the time map'?

- What danger does Joe see? Is it to himself or to somebody else?

- What does the writer mean by 'the transformation was absolute'?

In this opening paragraph, issues are raised about time, about danger, and about being drawn into someone else's business, which the writer continues to explore in the rest of the book.

ACTIVITY 15

Look at the first two paragraphs of the set text you are studying.

1 How does the writer prepare readers for what is to come?

2 Are there any clues in the text like the ones in *Enduring Love*?

Prose used emotively

A writer may use language to move the reader or to draw out a sympathetic response, as well as to inform. David Guterson is a master of this technique.

In his novel *Snow Falling on Cedars*, Guterson presents the thoughts of the local reporter, Ishmael, who has not got over his love for a Japanese girl many years earlier, despite affairs with other women:

He slept with each for a few more weeks after deciding he wanted nothing to do with them – he slept with them angrily and unhappily and because he was lonely and selfish . . . He knew that when he asked them to walk out of his life he would be even lonelier than he'd been before, and so he waited for a few weeks, both times, just to have someone around at night, just to come inside someone, just to hear someone breathing under him while he moved his hips with his eyes shut. Then his father came down to the city because he was dying, and Ishmael forgot about women.

Guterson makes the reader aware of the impossibility for Ishmael of replacing his great love. He shows the intense loneliness of this man because he wants the reader, at this point in the novel, to understand how Ishmael has suffered and still suffers.

ACTIVITY 16

Work out the different ways in which Guterson presents the feelings of Ishmael. You may include:

• repetition of 'lonely/lonelier'

• repetition of 'just'

• why the author mentions that Ishmael's eyes are shut

• how much Ishmael knows about himself

• his relationship with his father

• whether you feel any conflict of responses to Ishmael.

Lyrical prose

Lyrical prose is often used to establish a positive atmosphere in literature. It is prose which is poetic in its force, using the sorts of devices which you looked at earlier in this section. In this extract from *Things Fall Apart,* Chinua Achebe paints a picture of life in an African village, where a young boy, Nwoye, is growing up and has to spend more time with his father, Okonkwo, than with his mother:

> So Okonkwo encouraged the boys to sit with him in his *obi,* and he told them stories of the land – masculine stories of violence and bloodshed. Nwoye knew that it was right to be masculine and to be violent, but somehow he still preferred the stories that his mother used to tell, and which she no doubt still told to her younger children – stories of the tortoise and his wily ways, and of the bird *eneke-nti-oba* who challenged the whole world to a wrestling contest and was finally thrown by the cat.
>
> ---
> **obi* is the living quarters of the head of the family.

In this passage you realise that the boy has passed from childhood to youth; he has to leave the innocent folk-tales of his mother and listen to the war-like stories of his father. You feel sympathy for the young boy as he seems almost unwilling to grow up and would still prefer to be with his mother. Achebe describes briefly two of the myths told in the village. This gives a sense of the innocence and simplicity of traditional African village life, which is about to be wrecked by the arrival of the missionaries with their more modern beliefs: a whole culture is about to disappear.

David Guterson has also been acclaimed for the lyrical, poetic quality of his prose in *Snow Falling on Cedars.* In this extract, Ishmael goes to visit his elderly widowed mother:

> Ishmael's mother had the woodstove in the kitchen going – he could see the smoke rising thick from the chimney, a ghostly white against the hard-falling snow – and was standing at the sink in her overcoat and scarf when Ishmael passed in front of her window carrying his can of kerosene. A fog of condensation had formed on the inside of the pane, so that her image appeared to him as a kind of silhouette, a vague impression of his mother at the sink, refracted and fragmented, a wash of color.
>
> ---
> **refracted* means the effect of light seen at different angles.

ACTIVITY 17

The writer presents a vision of Ishmael's mother as though she were in a photograph or a painting. How does he create these effects? Consider:

- the use of words related to photography, such as 'refracted'

- the use of words related to painting, such as 'impression' and 'wash of color'

- words which suggest haziness

- words which suggest stillness

- words which suggests ghostliness

- the effects produced on you as a reader by this description.

Surreal prose

'Surreal' means the presentation of a character or scene as though it were in a dream, and not as you would perceive it in everyday life. Many modern writers use surreal effects in their work. Iris Murdoch, in her novel *The Bell*, achieves this effect in the account of Dora and Toby making love and rolling in the bell which seems to swallow them. In *Catch-22*, Joseph Heller creates many surreal effects, such as a picture of the hero Yossarian naked up a tree. In *One Flew Over the Cuckoo's Nest*, Ken Kesey creates a series of surreal pictures as he presents situations though the eyes of an 'insane' Indian Chief.

The following example of surreal prose is from Angela Carter's novel *The Magic Toyshop*. The central character, Melanie, is acting in a puppet show which is similar to *Swan Lake*. The male swan, a grotesque puppet, approaches her:

The swan made a lumpish jump forward and settled on her loins. She thrust with all her force to get rid of it but the wings came down all around her like a tent and its head fell forward and nestled in her neck. The gilded beak dug deeply into the soft flesh. She screamed, hardly realising she was screaming. She was covered completely by the swan but for her kicking feet and screaming face. The obscene swan had mounted her.

ACTIVITY 18

What do you think is going on in this scene? You need to consider:

- what the swan 'does' to her

- words which have sexual connotations such as 'loins', 'thrust', 'dug deeply' and 'mounted'.

  What is the effect of using these words? What could the word 'beak' suggest? Why is the beak 'gilded'?

Satirical prose

In **satirical prose**, the writer aims to attack society by ridiculing problems within it. This technique is employed by modern writers such as Alison Lurie. In her novel *The Last Resort*, Lurie satirises or mocks the behaviour of the residents and tourists in Key West, in Florida. She focuses on the vanity, greed and pretensions of the residents, and the wide-eyed naivety of the tourists. In this extract, one of the residents, Molly, is complaining about the tourist train which allows visitors to gawp at the residents and invade their privacy.

'She was very eager to go,' said Molly, who had never been on the train, though it passed her house continually. The day she and her husband first moved in, the loudspeaker had called the tourists' attention to a large tropical tree with loose, flaky bark that grew in their side yard. 'On your left, just ahead, you will see a fine specimen of one of Key West's native trees. It is a gumbo limbo, but natives call it the tourist tree, because it is always red and peeling.'

The first time Molly and her husband heard this joke they laughed . . . [*But they tire of the joke and try to get the commentary stopped.*] . . . Polite calls to the Conch Train office over the next few weeks accomplished nothing; the woman who answered the phone appeared to think that Molly should feel honored to have her tree noticed.

*Conch is a type of shellfish which the first residents of Key West fished for a living and ate.

ACTIVITY 19

Try to analyse this extract, picking out the attitudes that are being satirised. You could include:

- the attitude of Molly and her husband

- the attitude of the guide towards the tourists, including the dialogue of the commentary

- what this commentary implies about the visiting tourists

- the attitude of the lady from the Conch Train office.

Factual prose

Many modern writers incorporate factual language into their novels to create an effect. In her novel *Knowledge of Angels*, Jill Paton Walsh uses this style when she describes the torturing of the 'heretical atheist' Palinor:

Prisoner shown the devices.

DIXIT[†] INQUISITOR[*]	'Do you wish to confess?'
PRISONER	'What have I to confess? What have I done?'
INQ.	'You know what you have done.'

[*Prisoner stripped and bound.*]

INQ.	'Do you wish to confess?'
PRISONER	'What would you have me say?'
INQ.	'That you have known God from your first hours, and that you have perfidiously deserted him.'
PRISONER	'I will not confess that. It is not true.'

[*Cordeles and garrotes*** applied to prisoner.*]

INQ.	'Confess. We will release you at once if you confess.'
PRISONER	'No.'

[*Three turns. Prisoner voids his bowels. Prisoner screams.*]

---

*The *inquisitor* is a member of a team like the Spanish inquisitors who tortured many non-believers in the Catholic faith.

†*dixit* is Latin for 'says'.

***Cordeles* and *garrotes* are thin ropes used for strangulation.

ACTIVITY 20

What effects does the writer create by using this prose style for this account? You need to consider:

- the dramatic effects, as this reads like a play script

- whether you feel distanced from the scene and why

- whether you take in the details of the torture in a clear way

- what you feel for and about the victim

- whether the cold, factual details tell you something about the minds of those who impose the torture.

Here the writer provides the reader with stark details, offering precise and accurate information. In most of the book Walsh writes lyrically and delicately, as you saw on page 7. Why do you think that she varies the style like this? Here are some possible reasons:

- The variety of prose style keeps the reader interested.

- The clear account of the torture creates a picture in the reader's mind which is shocking and powerful.

- The change to 'official' information gives us a sense that the writer knows what she is talking about.

- This gives the text a sense of historical authenticity.

Mixing prose styles

You have seen the use of mixed prose styles, and have considered why the writer did this. This technique is also used by other contemporary writers, such as Sebastian Faulks in his novel *Birdsong*. Here, Faulks is writing about the horrors of the First World War and he offers a factual account of the work of those who dug the tunnels:

> Jack Firebrace lay forty-five feet underground with several hundred thousand tons of France above his face. He could hear the wooden wheezing of the feed that pumped air through the tunnel. Most of it was exhausted by the time it reached him. His back was supported by a wooden cross, his feet against the clay, facing towards the enemy. With an adapted spade, he loosened quantities of soil into a bag which he passed back to Evans, his mate, who then crawled away into the darkness.

The style here seems to be **detached** or **objective**, with Faulks conveying facts rather than emotions. The writer gives clear details of the depth at which the men work, and of the dangerous nature of the work which the tunnellers undertake. Faulks here chooses to let the facts speak for themselves. Elsewhere, the style changes when he tries to draw an engaged, emotional response from his readers. An example of this is the incident when a recovery party goes in search of the men killed in an underground explosion. They find the bodies of the men:

> Bright and sleek on liver, a rat emerged from the abdomen; it levered and flopped fatly over the ribs, glutted with pleasure. Bit by bit on to stretchers, what flesh fell left in mud. Not men, but flies and flesh, thought Stephen. Brennan anxiously stripping a torso with no head. He clasped it with both hands, dragged legless up from the crater, his fingers vanishing into buttered green flesh. It was his brother.

ACTIVITY 21

1 Work in groups and analyse the ways in which the language works to express meaning in the first extract.

2 Repeat this exercise for the second extract.

3 Compare and contrast the differences in the language used in each extract.

4 Discuss what effects the writer has achieved by varying the styles of his prose writing.

Impressionistic prose

The impressionistic style was important in the development of the twentieth-century novel. Virginia Woolf and James Joyce were two writers who used an impressionistic style. This extract from *Mrs Dalloway* by Virginia Woolf is a good example:

> Mrs Dalloway said she would buy the flowers herself.
>
> For Lucy had her work cut out for her. The doors would be taken off their hinges; Rumpelmayer's men were coming. And then, thought Clarissa Dalloway, what a morning – fresh as if issued to children on a beach.
>
> What a lark! What a plunge! For so it had always seemed to her when, with a little squeak of the hinges, which she could hear now, she had burst open the French windows and plunged at Bourton into the open air. How fresh, how calm, stiller than this of course, the air was in the early morning; like the flap of a wave; the kiss of a wave . . .

This extract comes from a series of impressions from within the mind of the main character, Clarissa Dalloway. The facts are limited:

- she is going to have a party

- preparations are already underway

- she has had parties like this before.

But how important are those facts? Are they the main point of the passage? Probably the answer is no. The originality here lies in the ways in which we are offered Mrs Dalloway's thoughts as she thinks them. This technique is called **stream of consciousness**. It works on a variety of levels.

- You see that Mrs Dalloway enjoys life and is enthusiastic.

- You get to know her by the use of images which are the key to her way of thinking – images of the beach and of the sea, the words 'fresh' and 'flap' and 'kiss', all positive words of enjoyment and movement.

- The senses are used to convey the feelings more powerfully.

- You also go into a flashback to the past at Bourton.

- The prose has been written in such a way as to convey the thoughts of the woman as they occur in a series of impressions. And it is these thoughts that give us a glimpse into the mind of Mrs Dalloway that are important, rather than any narrative development of plot.

ACTIVITY 22

Try to write out the extract above in a traditional narrative sequence. Try to work out the key images which Virginia Woolf uses, and consider the effects of these.

Prose of psychological analysis

Like the impressionistic style, this writing style also looks inwards, into the mind of the character. Again, this is one of the main developments in twentieth-century prose. In this extract from *The Sea*, *The Sea* by Iris Murdoch, the central character, Charles Arrowby, narrates his own story. He frequently pauses in the narrative account to share his thoughts with the reader. In this extract, he has just met an old girlfriend whom he thinks he has treated badly:

I am moved by having seen Lizzie and am wondering whether I have been clever or foolish. Of course if I had taken poor Lizzie in my arms it would all have been over in a second. At the moment when she hurled her handbag away she was ready to give in, to make every concession, to utter every promise. And how much I wanted to seize her. This ghost embrace remains with me as a joy mislaid. (I must admit that, after having seen her, my ideas are a good deal less 'abstract'!) Yet perhaps it was wise, and I feel satisfied with my firmness.

ACTIVITY 23

There is a lot going on in this passage. Try to work out some of the effects which Murdoch creates. You could include:

- the character of Charles . . . is he a little bit arrogant?

- the character Charles's relationship with the reader

- his language, e.g. 'joy mislaid', is he slightly stuffy or formal or old-fashioned?

The actual meeting of Lizzie and Charles occurs earlier in the book. Now you can see it from another perspective. Iris Murdoch has created a style and approach which allows you to see people and situations from multiple perspectives, so that there is a 'rounded' view and you are not forced to accept one viewpoint.

As a result, in Iris Murdoch's writing, like that of Virginia Woolf, we are given character studies of greater depth than in many other types of novel.

The next extract is written in the traditional third person and is a narrative account from Michael Dibdin's novel, *The Long Finish*, a detective story. The chief suspect, Minot, is about to be arrested for the second time on suspicion of murder:

That first time, the evening before, Minot had just finished eating a bowl of the lentil soup he made every Sunday, and which sat in its cauldron on the stove for the rest of week. Eating lentils made you rich, his father had told him; every one you swallowed would come back one day as a gold coin . . .

When he'd finished eating, Minot sluiced out the bowl under the tap and left it to dry. Then he went next door, sat down and turned on the television . . . He could only get two channels . . . but Minot didn't care. He wasn't interested in any of the programmes anyway. He just liked having the set on. It made the room more lively.

ACTIVITY 24

Rewrite this extract from the viewpoint of Minot in the style of either Virginia Woolf or Iris Murdoch, trying to use the sort of language that you think your chosen writer would make her character use.

In this section you have considered various types of narrative prose writing: emotive, lyrical, surreal, satirical, prose involving the use of accurate, factual language, impressionistic prose writing and prose of psychological analysis.

You have now looked at form in the novel, and types of writing within that form. To complete the work on the third Assessment Objective, the following section will cover structure and structural devices.

Structure and structural devices

Structure is *not* the same thing as narrative sequence. 'Structure' means the ways in which the writer makes all the different elements of the book hang together or fuse into a coherent whole. Structure and structural devices are the ways in which the writer imposes unity on his/her novel.

You need to consider some of the most important ways of achieving this unity by exploring the following structural devices:

- appendices

- epilogue

- continuous narrative

- dialogue

- narrative viewpoint: first- or third-person narration, the viewpoint of a child, split narrative account and the use of letters.

- setting

- repetition and repetitive motifs

- handling of time: flashback and time shifts.

Appendices

Sometimes at the end of the narrative sequence of a novel, when the plot has run its course, the writer may add an appendix or some appendices. Normally the word refers to sections added on to the end of a book; some writers use appendices to create a particular effect on the structure and therefore the meanings of the whole book.

Ian McEwan attaches two appendices at the end of his novel *Enduring Love*. In the main section of this novel the reader has been offered an account of an obsessive love which one of the characters, Jed, has developed for the central character, Joe. The reader realises that Jed is mentally sick. The first appendix is a case history of patients suffering from a similar problem, de Clérambault's syndrome. The second appendix is a final letter from Jed to Joe. Both appendices are included for a specific purpose.

In the first appendix:

- The account of patients suffering from this illness may affect your response to the character Jed.

- You can now look back over the narrative and see things in a different light, so that the novel itself may be seen to change its nature and take on the form of a case history.

- There is a shift in the type of language used, as was discussed earlier in the writing of Jill Paton Walsh and Sebastian Faulks. The medical register may persuade you that the author knows what he is talking about.

- This also creates variety for the reader.

In the second appendix, McEwan offers a final letter, to give the reader some background information:

Letter collected from Mr J. Parry, written towards end of his third year after admittance. Original filed with patient's notes . . .

The letter concludes:

Thank you for loving me, thank you for accepting me, thank you for recognising what I am doing for our love. Send me a new message soon, and remember – faith is joy.

Jed

ACTIVITY 25

1 What do you think are the effects of this final letter?

2 How do you respond to Jed now? Does this affect your sympathies?

3 How do you respond to Joe now? Do you think that he may have contacted Jed? What do you think the future holds for Joe in his relationship with Jed?

4 Does Ian McEwan achieve a double-take here? Are your sympathies shifted back to Joe with the future problems he will face from Jed?

5 Do you think that in this way the events of the novel are projected beyond the actual end of the novel, as events are ongoing?

Epilogue

Sometimes the same effect is achieved by the use of an **epilogue,** often in the form of a direct address to the reader by the writer or one of the characters. In *Studies in the Park*, Anita Desai presents the narrator as he revisits the park where he went earlier to try to study, some years after the events described:

I went back to the park of course. But now I was changed. I had stopped being a student, I was a 'professional'. My life was dictated by the rules and routine of the park. I still had my book open on the palms of my hands as I strolled but now my eyes strayed without guilt . . . My father says I need help. He says I am hopeless but that I need help. I just laugh but I know that he knows I will never appear for the examination, I will never come up to that hurdle or cross it – life has taken a different path for me, in the form of a search, not a race as it is for him, for them.

ACTIVITY 26

What do you think may be the effect on the reader of this epilogue in relation to earlier events? You need to consider:

- the effect achieved, by getting to see the character later in life

- being able to see if there are any changes in the characters' attitudes

- being able to see things in a double perspective of past and present

- whether the epilogue throws any new light on to the outcomes of the story, either from the point of view of a character in the book or from the author directly.

Continuous narrative

Continuous narrative is the traditional style of writing novels or short stories in which events are developed in a logical, chronological sequence. Here you may well see a character's life in an apparently realistic time sequence. Most of our nineteenth-century novelists, such as Charles Dickens, Thomas Hardy or George Eliot wrote in this way. Some contemporary writers also use this method. Jill Paton Walsh, in her novel *Knowledge of Angels*, uses this form of narrative account to create a sense of the important historical events unfolding as a youth arrives on an island, establishes a controversial religion and dies a martyr:

Above the woods the mountain was almost sheer for thousands of feet, and they moved slowly on the narrow shelves that served for paths.

The style is detailed and apparently realistic. In her introduction to the book, Jill Paton Walsh explains how the knowledge of the reader is like that of angels:

. . . a hovering, gravely attentive presence, observing everything, from whom nothing is concealed . . .

ACTIVITY 27

Try to work out what the author means here, and why you think that she uses continuous prose.

Dialogue

Dialogue is very important in most novels, and is a very effective method for the writer to develop ideas.

Here is a short piece of dialogue from Sylvia Plath's novel *The Bell Jar*. The central character, Esther, who is the narrator, has had a breakdown. This is partly due to a bad relationship with her mother, and also to her father's death. She has been to the hospital for electric shock therapy and has decided to discharge herself. Her mother comes to collect her:

'I'm through with that Doctor Gordon,' I said, after we had left Dodo and her black wagon behind the pines. 'You can call him up and tell him I'm not coming next week.'

My mother smiled. 'I knew my baby wasn't like that.'

I looked at her. 'Like what?'

'Like those awful people. Those awful dead people at that hospital.' She paused. 'I knew you'd decide to be all right again.'

This short dialogue offers the reader a lot of information very succinctly, in particular about the mother.

- She has no idea of what Esther has suffered in and out of hospital.

- She has no idea why Esther cannot face more therapy.

- She clearly misunderstands the nature of mental illness.

- She sees this as a stigma – 'those awful dead people'.

- She obviously thinks that Esther has been play-acting – 'I knew you'd decide to be all right'.

- She does not know her daughter, her 'baby', at all, and does not seem to grasp or to care that Esther has suffered so much.

ACTIVITY 28

What do you think the extract reveals about Esther? You need to consider:

- her attempts to communicate with her mother

- what she realises about their relationship.

Think about what this short extract of dialogue achieves.

1 It reminds you of what has happened earlier.

2 It summarises accurately and briefly, the poor relationship between Esther and her mother.

3 It gives a surprisingly clear picture of the poor quality of the mothering offered to Esther.

4 The simplicity of the style helps the reader to know the speaker, Esther, and to get a picture of how she responds to people.

Here is a short piece of dialogue from Margaret Atwood's novel, *The Handmaid's Tale*. Two of the handmaids, the narrator Offred and Ofglen, are taking their usual walk:

'I'd like to pass by the church,' says Ofglen, as if piously.

'All right,' I say, though I know as well as she does what she's really after.

We walk, sedately.

Atwood has passed on quite a lot of information very economically in this conversation. Think about:

- why the exchanges are so brief

- the relationship that is evident between the two women

- why Margaret Atwood uses the phrase 'as if piously'

- what this suggests about the character of Offred

- why the author offers another perspective on the dialogue by having Offred explain what she thinks is going on in Ofglen's head

- why the woman wants to pass 'by' but not 'in' the church?

ACTIVITY 29

Select a piece of dialogue from the text which you are studying, or use the extract below. Using the models above, analyse how the dialogue is used to convey important ideas, and discuss the style in which it is written.

This is a second extract from *The Handmaid's Tale*. Offred has gone to a night club with an officer:

'Well?' he says. 'What do you think of our little club?' . . .

'It's a club?' I say.

'Well, that's what we call it, among ourselves. The club.'

'I thought this sort of thing was strictly forbidden,' I say.

'Well, officially,' he says. 'But everyone's human, after all.' . . .

'What does that mean?'

'It means you can't cheat Nature,' he says. 'Nature demands variety, for men.'

Narrative viewpoint

Narrative viewpoint is the point of view from which the writer allows the reader to see events in the text. There are several ways of varying this, including first-person narration, third-person narration, the use of a child's viewpoint, split narrative and the use of letters.

First-person narration

This is used when the central character or one of the other characters is telling the story through his or her own eyes. Margaret Atwood uses first-person narration in her novel *The Handmaid's Tale*, where the narrative account begins and ends with Offred speaking to the reader directly:

> We slept in what had once been the gymnasium . . . A balcony ran around the room, for the spectators, and I thought I could smell, faintly like an afterimage, the pungent smell of sweat . . .

This achieves certain effects:

- the reader feels close to the person telling the story

- you build up a relationship with this character

- you recognise her language, which gives the book unity of tone.

But it is important to be aware that in those books which use first-person narration, writers often incorporate other devices to offer different viewpoints so that too much is not seen from one point of view.

Writing in the first person allows the reader to see into the minds of characters as they are in the process of thinking. Sometimes this technique is known as **interior monologue**. You have already looked at an example of this on page 20 in Iris Murdoch's presentation of the thoughts of Charles Arrowby in *The Sea, The Sea*. An interior monologue is often used by writers to vary viewpoints using third-person narrative.

Third-person narration

This is the standard form of many novels in which the writer is recounting the lives of the characters. Take, for example, Jill Paton Walsh's novel *Knowledge of Angels*. Although this is written in third-person narrative, we are frequently given glimpses into the minds of various characters. In this extract we are shown Beneditx's thoughts about the creation of the world:

He saw visions of angels at work in every moment of creation. Their hands flexed the tops and branches of the trees to raise the wind; their hands carried each single snowflake in the myriad storms and laid it softly down; their delicate fingers unfurled the scrolled leaves on the fig trees and silently opened each blossom on the almond boughs.

ACTIVITY 30

What does this extract tell us about the character of Beneditx here? You need to consider:

- what Beneditx believes about the nature of creation

- what sort of a person you think Beneditx is

- the way he pictures these things in his mind

- the sort of language the writer uses to describe these inner visions

- how and why this extract contrasts with the episode of torture you saw on page 17.

As you can see, Jill Paton Walsh lets us know exactly what is going on in Beneditx's head. In fact, using the third-person narrative technique gives her great freedom, because she does not have to write in the voice of one character all the time, or use the same register throughout; she can control her characters in a god-like way.

ACTIVITY 31

Now examine your chosen text, and decide which narrative form the writer has chosen to use. If it is the third-person form, look carefully through the book for any instances where you think that the writer has intervened to break the narrative account and lead the reader into forming an opinion.

Writing from the viewpoint of a child

Writing from a child's viewpoint is another way of creating interesting effects in prose texts. L. P. Hartley uses this technique in his novel *The Go-Between*. In this extract, the central character, Leo, is dragged along by the lady of the manor, Mrs Maudsley, until he sees his 'friends' having sex:

Not a sound came from the forlorn row of huts; only the rain pattering on their battered roofs. I could not bear to aid her in her search, and shrank back, crying. 'No, you *shall* come,' she said, and seized my hand, and it was then that we saw them, together on the ground, the Virgin and the Water-Carrier, two bodies moving like one. I think I was more mystified than horrified; it was Mrs. Maudsley's repeated screams that frightened me, and a shadow on the wall that opened and closed like an umbrella.

*The *Virgin* and the *Water-Carrier* are two signs of the Zodiac.

ACTIVITY 32

Work out the ways in which the writer achieves his effects in this extract. You need to think about:

- the use of adjectives like 'forlorn' and 'battered'

- the use of punctuation

- the attitude of the child who is 'crying', 'mystified' and 'frightened'

- the innocence of the child, with his image of the 'umbrella'

- the awareness of the reader compared to that of the child.

Split narrative account

Some writers may use split narrative account, where the story is told through the eyes and voice of more than one speaker. An example of this is Graham Greene's novel, *The End of the Affair*. In this novel, Greene writes about the problems of the Catholic religion. The two central characters, Bendrix and Sarah, are having an affair. They are together when a bomb drops on their building and it looks as though Bendrix has been killed. Sarah prays and promises God that if her lover were to survive, she would end the affair. The reader sees the first part of the book through Bendrix's eyes; he is hurt, baffled and bewildered because Sarah has left him. Then in the second part the same events are seen through Sarah's eyes; Greene reveals why she made the pact, and why she cannot continue the affair. Some of the advantages of this technique are listed below.

1 The reader always knows more than the characters do about what is going on, which is a form of **dramatic irony**. Therefore the reader is always in a better position than the characters themselves to understand situations.

2 You get to know the minds of the characters very intimately.

3 It also provides great unity of actions, characters and events so that the novel hangs together very tightly as there is always an overview.

ACTIVITY 33

Rewrite an episode from your set text through the eyes of another character. You need to consider how a character is established and defined:

- by what a character says

- by what a character does

- by noting any difference between what a character says and what a character actually does

- by noting how other characters react to this character

- by looking at the language the author uses in his account of this character: is it positive or negative?

- by analysing the dialogue put into that character's mouth

- by analysing any interior monologue which that character engages in.

ACTIVITY 34

Using the checklist above, compile a character study from your set text. Look again at any character studies which you may have compiled earlier.

Letters

Using letters is another way of varying the viewpoint in a story. You have already seen on page 4 a reference to a novel, *The Color Purple*, by Alice Walker, which is written in the form of letters. On page 23 the novel *Enduring Love* by Ian McEwan concludes with a letter from one character to another. The use of letters allows the reader to see events from different angles.

Setting

Setting is always important in establishing the structure of a novel or short story. You become familiar with the settings, especially if they are revisited throughout the book. In this way you gain an understanding of a character's relationship with the setting in which the writer places him/her.

Sometimes the setting is described vividly to give a feeling of reality to the book, as in this example from Iris Murdoch's novel *The Bell*, where one of the characters, Dora, goes out into the gardens:

They went on down to the causeway. This crossed the lake in a series of shallow arches built of old brick which had weathered to a rich blackish red. Each arch with its reflection made a dark ellipse. Dora noticed that the centre of the causeway was missing and had been replaced by a wooden section standing on piles.

Here the reader is offered a clear picture of the lake in the gardens of the community's home. There is a sense of richness in the idea of the brick 'weathering', it seems solid and secure. There is a vivid reflection in the water, which suggests stillness and tranquillity. You have a sense of deep colours, black and red brick, but the author does more than establish a sense of place here; this setting is to become central in the later dramatic events of the novel. Iris Murdoch uses setting to echo events, with red and black foreshadowing murder and passion later on.

When a writer establishes settings, they are usually more than a mere backdrop to events. Often they are used to remind the reader of the issues within the book. Here are two examples from David Guterson's novel, *Snow Falling on Cedars*. Carl Heine, a solid and steady fisherman, has been killed or murdered. One of the central issues of the book revolves around the trial of the murder suspect, Kabuo Miyamato. The writer gives a description of Carl Heine's home seen through the eyes of a reporter:

> It was precisely the sort of home Carl *would* build, he thought – blunt, tidy, gruffly respectable, and offering no affront to the world, though at the same time inviting nobody . . . Carl had cleared the land himself with characteristic rapidity . . . He'd wanted inglenooks, somebody had said, and an overscaled fireplace and alcoves, built-in window seats . . . But in time, as he worked, he'd found himself too straightforward for all of that . . . What he ended up with was a blunt, sturdy house sheathed carefully with cedar shingles, testimony to its builder's exacting nature.

ACTIVITY 35

1 What do you learn from this description of setting?

2 How much is this an account of the house or of the owner?

3 What sort of person is Carl? Look at the key words which relate to him, beginning with the second line and then working through the extract.

4 How might the writer be using this account to gain the reader's sympathy during the trial?

Setting is used here as a shorthand to develop the reader's perception of the character of a dead man, and to manipulate sympathy.

Elsewhere in the novel Guterson describes the setting for one of the days of the trial:

The storm winds battered the courtroom windows and rattled them in their casements so vigorously it seemed the glass would break . . . They had not at all grown accustomed to it . . . The snow was one thing, falling as it did, but the whine of the storm, the stinging force of it against their faces – everyone wished unconsciously that it would come to an end and grant them peace.

ACTIVITY 36

What do you think the storm suggests in this extract? How is it used to indicate:

- the hardship of life for the community

- the disturbance externally and internally caused by the trial?

Setting can also be used to establish a mood. In the following extract from William Trevor's novel, *Death in Summer*, one of the central characters, Thaddeus Davenant, is remembering the setting of his wife's funeral:

All that is over now, and yet is coldly there in the first moment of waking every day: the coffin, the flowers laid out, the bright white surplice of the clergyman, dust to dust . . . The day the heatwave began it was, that funeral afternoon, the empty blue of the sky touched upon in the clergyman's brief eulogy . . .

The writing is deceptively clear and artless. The key aspects of the funeral scene occur in a series of brief memory-flashes: the sky, an 'empty blue', economically tells us of Thaddeus's feelings after his wife's death, as he feels empty also. The weather echoes his feelings on the day of her funeral. Even the word order 'The day the heatwave began it was', is rather jumbled as befits a man whose mind is troubled.

At the same time the writer is deliberately misleading the reader, lulling us into an unthinking acceptance of what the scene we are reading shows. In fact, the mood is soon reversed as a murder is uncovered. In this example, setting is used to set up a deception, to surprise and shock the reader.

ACTIVITY 37

Now make a list of the various settings in your text, and try to analyse their significance.

Repetition and repetitive motifs

Just as settings begin to have associations for you as you read through a novel, many writers can use repetition or repetitive motifs for the same purpose, to emphasise in shorthand the key themes of the novel or short story.

A **motif** is like a refrain that recurs in music, and can form a series of images or symbols which occurs throughout a text. Here are a few examples:

- In her novel *The Handmaid's Tale* Margaret Atwood uses flowers as a motif. Each time they are described you learn something about the handmaid's state of mind. Blue irises evoke ideas of vitality and of freedom; the red tulips bring associations of death and isolation. When the handmaid has begun her relationship with Nick the flowers are 'of high summer: daisies, black-eyed Susans, starting us on the long downward slope to fall'. This parallels the life of the handmaid herself, caught up in an unstoppable train of events.

- Jill Paton Walsh uses the phrase 'knowledge of angels' as a motif in her novel of the same title. This recurs throughout the book, each time slightly redefined as the reader's own perceptions of the limitations of human knowledge and of human tolerance grow.

ACTIVITY 38

Check through your set text to see if this technique is being used by the writer. If it is, work out the sequence of motifs, and the associations which they carry for you. Here are some examples:

- the use of toys and gadgets in *The Magic Toyshop*

- references to the colour red in *The Handmaid's Tale*

- references to snow and to nature in *Snow Falling on Cedars*.

The handling of time

The handling of time is a tricky matter for writers of novels and short stories. It is straightforward in novels where time is realistic and follows a natural chronological sequence. How does a writer of other types of prose move backwards and forwards through time? There are two interesting ways of doing this: the use of flashbacks, and the use of time-shift.

Flashback

This is a straightforward concept, when a character reminisces about events that have happened in the past. The writer can then take us backwards in time without disturbing the flow of the narrative. In the following example from the novel *The Child in Time* by Ian McEwan, the central character, Stephen, glances through the window of a pub and sees two people inside:

> But the young man and women were engrossed. He gulped his beer, a pint to her half, and talked earnestly, while her drink remained untouched . . . His legs weakened, a chill spread downwards through his stomach. He was looking into the eyes of the woman, and he knew who she was . . . There was no response from the young woman who he knew, beyond question, was his mother. She could not see him. She was listening to his father speak . . .

This is a flashback, but presented in dramatic terms as a real experience. Stephen is made to confront his past imaginatively, but also as if it had really happened. The window he looks through is not just the pub window, it is the window of time. He sees his parents when they were young, before he had been conceived. It is as if the writer is telling us that the past is always with us.

In his novel *Catch-22*, Joseph Heller uses flashback in a complex way. The central character of the novel, Yossarian, appears to be mentally ill when you first encounter him. He does not want to return to war as a bombardier, he may even be cowardly. Heller introduces a series of flashbacks which Yossarian has, related to the death of his fellow crew-member Snowden. As the sequence of the same flashback builds up, you begin to realise that there is something important hidden here. In the final flashback of the sequence near the end of the book, the reader is presented with the grim details of Snowden's death:

> Yossarian ripped open the snaps of Snowden's flak suit and heard himself scream wildly as Snowden's insides slithered down to the floor in a soggy pile and just kept dripping out.

ACTIVITY 39

Try to work out the effects achieved by this flashback. You need to consider:

- how this flashback might affect your response to Yossarian

- the reason for Yossarian's state of mind

- how Heller uses language to achieve particular effects.

Time-shift

Time-shift is a similar device to flashback but it works in a slightly different way and for slightly different purposes. At the end of Kate Atkinson's novel *Behind the Scenes at the Museum*, for example, Ruby Lennox revisits the shop in York, which is now a café, where she spent so much time in her childhood. She glances out of the window:

From one of the newly-genteel lace-curtained windows I can see a wild scene in the street below – the stomping, disciplined marching of thousands of feet as a Roman army marches up from the river, through the *porta praetoria* and along the street. The plumes on the centurions' helmets tremble, the standard bearers hold their standards proudly aloft.

Without warning, still in the present tense, we have slipped over a thousand years back in time. The point that Atkinson is making is that this is what life is; we all arrive, live and then disappear into the museum of history. The only problem with this technique is that on first reading it can be confusing, but it is a vivid and dramatic way of including the past in a novel.

This sort of confusion is also evident on a first reading of Toni Morrison's novel *Beloved*. Here time-shift is used to move backwards and forwards through time and history, as the writer explores the damage caused by slavery to people of a later generation. One of the central parts of the novel involves time-shift as the reader discovers the guilty secret of the central character, Sethe.

When the four horsemen came – schoolteacher, one nephew, one slave catcher and a sheriff – the house on Bluestone Road was so quiet they thought they were too late . . .

Inside, two boys bled in the sawdust and dirt at the feet of a nigger woman holding a blood-soaked child to her chest with one hand and an infant by the heels in the other. She did not look at them; she simply swung the baby towards the wall planks, missed and tried to connect a second time . . .

ACTIVITY 40

Using the extract from *Beloved*, try to work out the effects of the sudden time-shift. You should include:

- the dramatic effect achieved by the writer's use of language

- the economy of being able to avoid lengthy chronological narrative prose

- the development of the writer's ideas

- how it makes the episode seem more real and vivid.

ACTIVITY 41

Look again at your set text and see how the writer treats past events. Perhaps there is a mixture of devices used. If so, what effect does each one have?

ACTIVITY 42

Having covered all the areas relating to the third Assessment Objective, now try to answer these general questions about the prose style of the set text you are reading.

1 Is the style clear or complex?

2 Is the writing subjective or objective?

3 Is the style traditional or modern or experimental?

4 How is word order and pacing treated?

5 How is dialogue used?

6 Is there much use of figurative language? What effect does this produce?

7 Does the work contain impressionistic writing or psychological analysis?

8 How is the past handled?

9 What form of narrative account is used?

You should now be able to respond fully to the three questions which relate to the first three Assessment Objectives:

• What ideas is the writer trying to convey to his readers?

• What is the experience or experiences which the writer is trying to convey?

• How is he/she trying to convey these ideas and experiences?

The final section of this module looks at the requirements of Assessment Objective 4. At this stage in your studies, the primary text is the most important thing. You will not be expected to spend too much study time reading 'secondary' texts, that is, critical texts that discuss your chosen novel, books of literary theory, or books which consider different readings of your text.

AO4: articulate independent opinions and judgements

Your work on this objective should be focused on two key areas:

1 The formulation of your own independent opinion about the set text

2 The awareness that there may be ambiguity in the text, and that you will formulate a reading which may be personal to you.

1 How to be an informed, independent reader

In the exam you might be asked questions in the form: 'What do you find interesting in . . . ?' or 'What is the significance of . . . ?' or 'How important is . . . ?'

It is important to realise that you are being asked for an opinion by your examiner. You must respond by offering an opinion or judgement. If you don't offer an opinion, or try to hedge your bets, for example, by saying 'I am not sure . . . ' or ' It is not clear . . . ', you will have failed to respond to the task set, and risk losing the marks to be gained under this objective. Try to be confident when you go into the exam that you do have a firm opinion about what the book means to you.

2 Awareness of ambiguity and formulating a personal reading

Remember that texts do not have one single meaning. The writer might have created deliberate ambiguity, or might have intended the reader to form a certain opinion. But when you, as a reader, come to the text, you bring a different set of experiences and a different set of associations to bear on your interpretation. You may well draw a different message from the text from that which the author intended.

Your interpretation is always acceptable as long as you can back it up with evidence from the text itself.

The following three extracts from Jill Paton Walsh's novel *Knowledge of Angels* offer examples of ambiguity. As you will see, the definition of 'knowledge' changes as the novel progresses:

> 'You speak of evening knowledge – knowledge of things as they are and have been in the visible world. I speak of morning knowledge – knowledge of things as they were created, things as they are meant to be. The knowledge of angels is of both these kinds at once, but in mankind there is a difference. Inborn knowledge of God is morning knowledge.'

The discussion about knowledge is central to the debate on theology in the book. Here Beneditx suggests that mankind can actually partake of the knowledge of angels in a certain way, because man is born with an awareness of God. Later in the book, Beneditx returns to his earlier definition:

> ' . . . evening knowledge is that by which things are known in their own nature, such as knowing that no line in the world is really straight. There is a problem over the knowledge of angels . . .
>
> In angels, is there any difference between morning and evening knowledge? . . . There are shadows in the morning and in the evening. In an angelic intellect, however, there are no shadows, for angels are very bright mirrors. . . '

The definition is then developed further. Brutal events occur in the novel, and the once-optimistic Beneditx is seen to become disillusioned:

> How high he had once aspired! He had desired the knowledge of angels, in whom there was no difference between morning knowledge and evening knowledge . . . like an angel he had sought a knowledge without shadows, holding up to the creation a very bright mirror. And now the mirror of his soul was so fouled and darkened that neither morning nor evening could be distinguished from the black onrush of night.

ACTIVITY 43

1 Try to work out how the definition has changed. You need to consider:

- the significance of the word 'shadows' in the second extract: does it suggest that the shadows may be the inevitable limitations of man's knowledge?

- could the shadows relate to sinfulness, which angels, unlike mankind, cannot know?

2 Look at the ways in which Jill Paton Walsh has added layers to the definition of the knowledge of angels. You should consider the ideas:

- that mankind has no right to expect to achieve this sort of knowledge

- that mankind is essentially too sinful to achieve it.

Another ambiguous aspect of this book is the three-in-a-bed sexual encounter between Palinor, Dolca and Joffre. On a first reading this seems out of keeping with the content and tone of the rest of the book. But your response to this as a reader may illustrate two of the central themes of this book:

- the need for tolerance and charitable love for fellow human beings

- how in the knowledge of angels there are no shadows. So it is only people conscious of sin who would see this episode as sinful.

ACTIVITY 44

Now select an episode from your set text and work in groups to discuss any ambiguities you can find.

• *A personal reading*

It is important to consider here that different readers or groups of readers will respond to texts differently. The publication of Salman Rushdie's book *The Satanic Verses* caused no problem to Christian readers, who saw it as a witty, satirical book. However, Islamic readers saw the book as a sacrilegious attack on the equivalent of the Bible, the Koran. Rushdie was branded as a heretic, and condemned to be killed by a member of the Islamic faith.

Interpretations of a book can also change over time. A fairly recent example is *The Child in Time* by Ian McEwan. This was published in 1987 and at the time it was seen as an exploration of childhood, of relationships with parents and friends, and of how the passing of time affects our perceptions of life. Initially the concern with treatment of time was of great interest to readers. However, in the years since its publication and the current preoccupation with 'sleaze' in politics, many readers now see the book as a satire on political life. In it McEwan mocks the childlike or self-serving behaviour of politicians; he also satirises the peculiar and irrational actions of obsessive members of a secret organisation called the Movement.

Finally, as part of your personal interpretation you need to be aware that an author may have some specific purpose in mind, for example, the main arguments of the book might be concerned with claims about the rights of women and their role in society.

• *A feminist reading*

During the course of this module you have looked at several examples of work which could be regarded as feminist writing, such as the novels of Alice Walker and Toni Morrison. Other feminist writers include Angela Carter and Margaret Atwood.

Angela Carter, in her novel *The Magic Toyshop*, may be seen to offer a feminist exploration of a young girl's rite of passage from adolescence to womanhood, when she becomes aware of her own sexuality as a source of power and a life-enriching experience. In her short-story sequence, *The Bloody Chamber*, Angela Carter rewrites traditional fairy-tales, giving them a feminist reading by criticising the stereotypical male attitudes which she believes lie behind these stories.

In *The Handmaid's Tale*, Margaret Atwood can be seen exploring the lives of women who are deprived of their rights and roles in life. The next two extracts from *The Handmaid's Tale* illustrate a woman's loss of rights in the society described by Offred.

> I wait, washed, brushed, fed, like a prize pig. Sometime in the eighties they invented pig balls, for pigs who were being fattened in pens . . . they liked to have something to think about . . .
>
> I wish I had a pig ball.

> I lie on my back, fully clothed except for the healthy white cotton underdrawers . . .
>
> My red skirt is hitched up to my waist, though no higher. Below it the Commander is fucking. What he is fucking is the lower part of my body. I do not say making love, because this not what he's doing.

ACTIVITY 45

How does Margaret Atwood reveal the low status of the female handmaid in these extracts? Look carefully at the ways in which she uses language and imagery.

It is not only female writers who defend the roles and value of women in society. Shakespeare, in his portrayal of women such as Portia in *The Merchant of Venice*, may be seen as upholding modern feminist values. In his novel *Catch-22*, Joseph Heller attributes positive values to women such as Nately's whore and the Nurse.

• A socialist or Marxist reading

These readings rest on attitudes to class structure and behaviour. You could apply a Marxist reading to David Guterson's novel *Snow Falling on Cedars*. In this novel, a respected member of the community has been killed suddenly. The book centres on the trial of the suspect, Kabuo Miyamoto. As you read this book you become aware of old frictions between the local American population and the Japanese immigrants. This is seen to stem from the Second World War. A Marxist would say that the war was originally caused by capitalist greed for conquest, and that this has disturbed and threatened to destroy the harmony of this small community despite the fact that it is many years since the war. The writer makes distrust of the Japanese clear when the dead man's wounds are examined:

> It was precisely the sort of lethal impression Horace had seen at least two dozen times in the Pacific war . . . The Japanese field soldier, trained in the art of *kendo*, or stick fighting, was exceptionally proficient at killing in this manner. And the majority of Japs, Horace recalled, inflicted death over the left ear, swinging in from the right.

ACTIVITY 46

How does Guterson reveal Horace's mistrust of the Japanese? You should look carefully at the language he uses.

• *A psychoanalytical reading*

This reading is based on a psychoanalysis of the subconscious mind. The novels of Iris Murdoch are open to this type of reading. Here are two extracts from *The Bell*. In the first extract, the reader is offered three different responses to the situation where a young man, Toby, has been forced to leave the community of Imber because of his relationship with Michael:

'Where's Toby now?' said Michael.

'I sent him home,' said James.

Michael jumped up from his chair. He wanted to shout and bang on the desk. He said quietly to James, 'You perfect imbecile.'

James explains:

And I thought he should go while he felt, as it were, that he'd got back to some sort of innocence . . .

Michael drummed on the window. James was quite right in a way. But his heart ached terribly for Toby, sent away now with all his imperfections on his head, loaded with guilt, and involved by James's solemnity in a machinery of sin and repentance with which he probably had no capacity to deal.

Toby writes a letter on his return to Oxford, bright and cheery. Iris Murdoch comments:

The full significance of the happenings at Imber had happily escaped Toby, and he had no retrospective curiosity about them now.

ACTIVITY 47

Analyse the different responses of the three men. Would it be fair to suggest that James and Michael see things only through their own eyes? That they impose their own responses on Toby?

Of course, one of the central interests in *The Bell* is the response of the different characters as they become part of the group and achieve varying degrees of self-knowledge, as Iris Murdoch makes clear:

Those who hope, by retiring from the world, to earn a holiday from human frailty, in themselves and others, are usually disappointed.

The central irony and source of ambiguity within the book is the reversal of characters' expectations about themselves and other people.

- ## *Several readings within a text*

Texts are open to multiple readings; here are some examples from David Guterson's novel *Snow Falling on Cedars*. You have already seen a Marxist reading of this text; here are four more possible readings:

1 a tale about seafaring, rich in the details of life in a fishing community

2 a parable about the need for forgiveness, trust and tolerance in a community, and the world at large

3 a moral fable as Ishmael struggles to act honourably towards Horace

4 a whodunnit. The writer makes references to this genre:

> 'You want to play Sherlock Holmes?' asked Horace. 'You going to play detective?'

The reader is provided with plenty of motives for the murder, which seem to imply the guilt of Miyamoto. But Guterson complicates this genre when Ishmael, the newspaper reporter and owner, thinks about the death of Carl Heine. He admits that the death could have been caused by an accident at sea and realises:

> *Nobody knows*, thought Ishmael . . . Or rather one person, he himself, knew this truth. That was the heart of it.

At this stage the reader realises that Miyamoto is innocent, just hours before the verdict is due.

Remember there are three aspects to consider when addressing Assessment Objective 4:

ACTIVITY 48

What do you think is the effect later in the novel, when suspense about the guilt of the suspect has been removed early on? How might a writer sustain the reader's interest?

ACTIVITY 49

Working in groups, discuss your own interpretations or readings of the text you are studying. Be careful to base all these readings on textual evidence.

Remember there are three aspects to consider when addressing Assessment Objective 4:

1 be confident in holding and expressing an opinion or judgement

2 be aware of ambiguities of meaning, character or situation in your text

3 be able to support your reading with close textual evidence.

Summary

To conclude your work on this module, here is a summary list of questions to help you to explore your set text:

• What ideas is the writer trying to convey to the reader?

• What experience or experiences is he/she trying to convey?

• How has he/she tried to convey these ideas and experiences?

• How do I respond to the writer's ideas?

• Do I agree with what the writer is saying?

• In what ways are the ideas original, or valuable or interesting?

• Does this text appeal to me? Why or why not?

• Can I support my reading(s) of the text?

Preparing for a closed book examination

It is important to know your text very well, as it is for all types of exam. A significant difference in a closed book examination is the way in which textual evidence is handled. There are four things to bear in mind:

1 You always need to support your arguments with textual evidence.

2 You do not need to learn large chunks of text off by heart.

3 Examiners will always be satisfied with short but relevant phrases for examples of style

   or

4 Examiners will be satisfied with close echoes of the text, as long as there is a clear indication as to exactly which part of the text you are using as evidence.

Module ② Shakespeare

This module carries 30% of the total marks for the AS course. The marks are divided amongst the Assessment Objectives like this:

ASSESSMENT OBJECTIVES

AO1 communicate clearly the knowledge, understanding and insight appropriate to literary study, using appropriate terminology and accurate and coherent written expression
(7% of the final AS mark; 3.5% of the final A level mark)

AO2i respond with knowledge and understanding to a literary text
(10% of the final AS mark; 5% of the final A level mark)

AO3 show detailed understanding of the ways in which writers' choices of form, structure and language shape meanings
(8% of the final AS mark; 4% of the final A level mark)

AO4 articulate independent opinions and judgements.
(5% of the final AS mark; 2.5% of the final A level mark)

Approaching Shakespeare for this module

You will already have studied Shakespeare, at both Key Stage Three and GCSE. At AS level you should understand more about Shakespeare's craft, and have the chance to explore and enjoy another play. Although you might look at some critics' opinions of Shakespeare in class, it's *your* opinions that count most, both in reading the play and in writing for the exam.

There are two ways of being assessed for this module: through a written examination paper or through coursework. If you choose the exam option, you have to choose from three texts named in the specification, initially *Twelfth Night*, *Antony and Cleopatra* and *The Taming of the Shrew*. If you choose to do coursework, you can choose any play by Shakespeare, subject to the restrictions outlined in the section on coursework (see page 55).

Whichever assessment route you choose, the most important thing to remember is that your writing has to address the Assessment Objectives for the module. Of course, a very wide range of tasks could be set by the examination board, or by your teacher, which would test your '*knowledge and understanding*' (AO2i) of the text you've chosen. You will also have to show '*understanding of the ways in which writers' choices of form, structure and language shape meanings*' (AO3), and '*articulate independent opinions and judgements*' (AO4) grounded in the text.

The first part of this section will deal with Assessment Objectives 3 and 4 – identifying and using choices of form, structure and language, and forming independent judgements. An understanding of these issues is important to your success whichever assessment option you take.

> **AO3: detailed understanding of the ways in which writers' choices of form, structure and language shape meanings**

The first thing to say here is that with Shakespeare, as with any other writer, it's the whole objective that's being looked at; in other words, you're not interested simply in what the choices *are*, but what they *do* – how they help the writer to create meanings. There's no point in writing about iambic pentameters or choices of imagery, unless you're explaining why the writer has made these decisions.

Form

All of Shakespeare's plays use the **iambic pentameter** as the dominant verse form, even when other verse forms are employed occasionally. 'Pentameter' means that there are five beats in the line, and 'iambic' means that in each beat, or foot, there are two syllables, with the stress falling on the second syllable. That means it is a ten-syllable line, with the stress falling on syllables 2, 4, 6, 8 and 10. The **metre** of the lines can make particular words significant.

As an example of a regular iambic pentameter, here's the opening line of *Henry IV Part I*:

> So **shaken** as we **are**, so **wan** with **care**

You can see that the stresses fall naturally on the syllables marked. Here are some lines from *Romeo and Juliet*:

JULIET 'Tis but thy name that is my enemy;
Thou art thyself, though, not a Montague.
What's Montague? it is nor hand, nor foot,
Nor arm, nor face, nor any other part
Belonging to a man. O! be some other name:
What's in a name? that which we call a rose
By any other name would smell as sweet;
So Romeo would, were he not Romeo call'd,
Retain that dear perfection which he owes
Without that title. Romeo, doff thy name;   10
And for that name, which is no part of thee,
Take all myself.

ROMEO   I take thee at thy word.
Call me but love, and I'll be new baptiz'd;
Henceforth I never will be Romeo.

Look at the stresses here, and notice how many times they fall on the word 'name' – the word is used six times, and each time it's hit by the beat. That's not all, though: stresses also fall on 'call', 'call'd', 'title', and 'baptiz'd', all of which point to the problem of names. The words 'thyself' and 'myself' are also used by Juliet, with the stress falling on 'self', and this is the heart of the matter – identity. After all, if Romeo were not a Montague, but instead Romeo Smith, there wouldn't be a problem. The point here is not that the iambic pentameters emphasise words about names, but that by doing it Shakespeare brings the problem of names and identity to the audience's attention – he's using form to shape meanings.

There's another use of form here, too. Romeo completes Juliet's line 'Take all myself' with 'I take thee at thy word'. Because the ten syllables should flow in an unbroken string, the actor playing Romeo must come in quickly with his line, to maintain it. The broken line is a stage direction, in effect. What's the purpose, though? Here, it might be at this moment that Romeo suddenly appears – Juliet hasn't known that he is present and listening to her. Surprise as well as urgency might be signalled.

Now read this extract, which is the continuation of the passage above.

JULIET	What man art thou, that, thus bescreen'd in night, So stumblest on my counsel?
ROMEO	By a name I know not how to tell thee who I am: My name, dear saint, is hateful to myself, Because it is an enemy to thee: Had I it written, I would tear the word.

ACTIVITY 1

1 Count the references to 'name' in the passage above, and discuss where the rhythm falls.

2 'Self' is stressed again. Which other words are stressed that refer to identity?

3 The last word stressed in the passage is 'word'– doubly emphasised because it's at the end of the line and is followed by a full stop. What is the 'word' which Romeo would 'tear'?

Although the basic line is the iambic pentameter, it's the variations in the pentameter which often show the writer at work, manipulating the form to bring something to the audience's attention. Later on in the play, for instance, when Romeo is having to face the real difficulty of who he is, he speaks this line:

> As if that name
> Shot from the deadly level of a gun . . .

'Name' is stressed again, but in the next line the beginning is irregular: the first syllable, 'Shot', has to be stressed. Because the rhythm is different, it leaps to the audience's attention. Why? What meaning is the playwright trying to express? The language suggests violence, and perhaps Romeo's mental disturbance is suggested by the irregularity, too. He's disturbed, so the rhythm of the language mirrors his state of mind.

Here's a very famous speech from *Hamlet*, where the speaker is also disturbed.

HAMLET   To be, or not to be: that is the question:
Whether 'tis nobler in the mind to suffer
The slings and arrows of outrageous fortune,
Or to take arms against a sea of troubles,
And by opposing end them? To die: to sleep;
No more; and, by a sleep to say we end
The heart-ache and the thousand natural shocks
That flesh is heir to, 'tis a consummation
Devoutly to be wish'd. To die, to sleep;
To sleep: perchance to dream: ay, there's the rub;   10
For in that sleep of death what dreams may come
When we have shuffled off this mortal coil,
Must give us pause. There's the respect
That makes calamity of so long life;
For who would bear the whips and scorns of time,
The oppressor's wrong, the proud man's contumely,
The pangs of dispriz'd love, the law's delay,
The insolence of office, and the spurns
That patient merit of the unworthy takes,
When he himself might his quietus make   20
With a bare bodkin? who would fardels bear,
To grunt and sweat under a weary life,
But that the dread of something after death,
The undiscover'd country from whose bourn
No traveller returns, puzzles the will,
And makes us rather bear those ills we have
Than fly to others that we know not of?
Thus conscience does make cowards of us all;
And thus the native hue of resolution
Is sicklied o'er with the pale cast of thought,   30
And enterprises of great pith and moment
With this regard their currents turn awry,
And lose the name of action. Soft you now!
The fair Ophelia! Nymph, in thy orisons
Be all my sins remember'd.

The speech is generally taken to be a pondering on the problems of suicide – but a study of the metre suggests that it is more than this.

ACTIVITY 2

1 Look at the first line. It starts off regularly enough, but how many syllables are there in the line? Then look at the next few lines. Where do you find the first regular line?

2 Now go through the whole speech, counting syllables and listening to stresses.

So far, you've been gathering evidence. Now you have to interpret it.

3 You've probably found some runs of regular lines – those beginning at 'But that the dread', for instance. What do you think the significance is of these? Might they reflect things which have passed through Hamlet's mind before, and he's simply rehearsing the arguments? Look at what he says in these lines, and consider if it's likely.

4 The irregular lines at the beginning of the speech are enough in themselves to suggest a disturbed state of mind – but disturbed about what? The words at the ends of the lines should give you a clue.

5 At line 8, 'consummation' draws attention to itself because of the irregular rhythm of the line. 'Consummation' seems to mean death, in this context, but it's an odd word to use; it is more usually employed in connection with sexual relations in marriage. Which of Hamlet's problems is being suggested here, do you think?

6 Now look at the end of the speech, when Ophelia appears. Why do you think it's irregular here?

Structure

Whichever play you are studying, there are bound to be some structural features to comment on, connected to the playwright's purposes. When you look at the Acts and Scenes in the play as a whole – where they take place, when they take place, in what order they take place, and so on – there are bound to be things to notice.

In *Antony and Cleopatra*, for instance, the action in the early part of the play constantly switches between Egypt and Rome. The audience is bound to compare the two settings, and with them the central characters in each setting, and their language. Structure can be a lot more subtle than this, though. Look at this passage from the end of Act 5 Scene 1 of *King Richard II*:

KING RICHARD II	Twice for one step I'll groan, the way being short,
	And piece the way out with a heavy heart.
	Come, come, in wooing sorrow let's be brief,
	Since, wedding it, there is such length in grief.
	One kiss shall stop our mouths, and dumbly part;
	Thus give I mine, and thus take I thy heart.
QUEEN	Give me mine own again; 'twere no good part
	To take on me to keep and kill thy heart.
	So, now I have mine own again, be gone,
	That I might strive to kill it with a groan. 10
KING RICHARD II	We make woe wanton with this fond delay:
	Once more, adieu; the rest let sorrow say. [*Exeunt.*]

You might have noticed that this is written in rhyming couplets. In fact, the last 24 lines of the scene are written in this way; this feature of form is part of the structure of the scene. The scene begins with the Queen arriving on the stage with attendants to wait for Richard on his way to prison, and almost certain death. At the end of the scene '*Exeunt*' means 'they go off', but staging decisions have to be made. It's natural for Richard to leave first – he's being taken to prison under guard, after all. This would leave the Queen alone, watching him leave before she departs, in another direction. In this case, the Queen's arrival and exit would bracket the scene – another feature of structure.

This moment is also important in the structure of the whole play. This scene is the first time in the play that the Queen and Richard have spoken together. Up to now she has been more of an observer than someone who acts. At the beginning of this scene, however, she challenges Richard to act, and clearly shows her love for him, which he is shown to return. By the end of Act 4, Richard has been deposed as King by Bolingbroke, and the audience may well feel that the deposition is deserved. If this perception is unaltered by the time he dies, the play may take on the tone of a morality play, rather than being a tragedy. In other words Shakespeare needs to create sympathy for Richard.

He does this in Act 5 in a number of ways, with the result that the audience feels affected by his death, which makes the play theatrically richer. Richard is shown to repent his extravagant actions, he fights for his life – and he is shown to be capable of love, and being loved. In this, the Queen is the first and most powerful tool. Shakespeare has them kiss twice in the lines above (you might like to work out exactly where) and as she stands stricken with grief for the man on his way to his death, she has a powerful effect on the audience. Her purpose in the play is, therefore, to act as a structural tool. Through her, Shakespeare *uses structure to shape meanings* about the play.

Language

Shakespeare uses many language techniques to shape meanings: imagery, sound, syntax and so on. Here is a reminder of some of the features which you might look for to see how they create meanings.

Language can help to define character. For example, here are the first eleven lines spoken on stage by Caliban, the offspring of a witch, who is kept in servitude by Prospero in *The Tempest*:

> CALIBAN   As wicked dew as e'er my mother brush'd
> With raven's feather from unwholesome fen
> Drop on you both! a south-west blow on ye,
> And blister you all o'er.
>
> [. . .]
>
>   I must eat my dinner.
> This island's mine, by Sycorax my mother,
> Which thou tak'st from me. When thou camest first,
> Thou strok'dst me and mad'st much of me; wouldst give me
> Water with berries in't; and teach me how
> To name the bigger light, and how the less,   10
> That burn by day and night . . .

There are a number of features to notice here, which help to establish Caliban's character. Caliban's first sentence is an exclamation and a curse, as is the second. The syntax is fairly simple. 'I must eat my dinner' is hardly complex, in thought or language. The **diction** – the choice of individual words by the writer – has two noticeable features. It is simple, as in the example above, and in words such as 'takest' and 'camest'. It reflects a simple mind, which struggles to find the words for sun and moon. The language is aggressive, too. 'Wicked', 'blister', and 'unwholesome' show this, while 'raven' and 'fen' are words which have associations with evil and corruption.

You might expect to look for **imagery** when you think about language, and there isn't much here; but that has implications in itself, suggesting that Caliban thinks too simply and literally to use figurative language. The opening comparison is probably literal, as is 'the bigger light and . . . the less'. 'I must eat my dinner' is actually a metaphor – Caliban is stating that he has to do what he is told, for fear of punishment. This is revealing in itself: Caliban's metaphor is drawn from a simple, basic activity.

From the same play, here are the opening words spoken by Miranda, Prospero's daughter:

MIRANDA   If by your art, my dearest father, you have
           Put the wild waters in this roar, allay them.
           The sky, it seems, would pour down stinking pitch,
           But that the sea, mounting to th' welkin's cheek,
           Dashes the fire out. O, I have suffer'd
           With those that I saw suffer: a brave vessel,
           Who had, no doubt, some noble creatures in her,
           Dash'd all to pieces. O, the cry did knock
           Against my very heart. Poor souls, they perish'd.
           Had I been any god of power, I would   10
           Have sunk the sea within the earth, or e'er
           It should the good ship so have swallow'd and
           The fraughting souls within her.

ACTIVITY 3

The language features in Miranda's speech form a sharp contrast with those chosen for Caliban.

- Look at the first sentence. This isn't a curse; what is it?

- The syntax, though not particularly complex, is different from Caliban's. Can you identify phrases which qualify feelings and ideas? What does this tell you about Miranda?

- The diction is a little less simple: 'welkin' and 'fraughting' are not words which Caliban might have used. The dominant tone, created by the diction, is very different. Beginning from 'my dearest father' in the first line, find the words which are strikingly different, in either meaning or association, from Caliban's aggression. Again, what does this reveal about Miranda?

- Identify any imagery used by Miranda. What does 'the cry did knock against my very heart' reveal about Miranda?

Language, then, is one of the means used by the playwright to reveal character. But sometimes the language might change, and in doing so reveal something more about the writer's concerns. In the case of Caliban, for instance, his speech in Act 3 Scene 2 beginning:

Be not afeard: the isle is full of noises,
Sounds and sweet airs, that give delight, and hurt not

shows a different side to him. His final words in the play, 'I'll be wise hereafter, and seek for grace' come rather out of the blue, but his words in his penultimate scene are revealing. 'Good my lord, give me thy favour still. Be patient', 'speak softly', and so on, sound more like Prospero's diction than Caliban's. If Shakespeare is suggesting a change in Caliban by this language, it is a significant one: patience and grace are key ideas in his last plays. Here he is using language (and structure) to express meanings central to his drama.

Language can also be used to make the audience aware of the playwright's concerns. The imagery of blood and darkness which runs through the text of *Macbeth*, for instance, is central to the play's meaning, as is the imagery of blindness in *King Lear*.

Here is a passage from Act 2 Scene 4 of *Macbeth*:

> Ross   Ah! good father,
> Thou seest, the heavens, as troubled with man's act,
> Threaten his bloody stage: by the clock 'tis day,
> And yet dark night strangles the travelling lamp.
> Is't night's predominance, or the day's shame,
> That darkness does the face of earth entomb,
> When living light should kiss it?

This speech, from a relatively minor character, and not in a crucial moment of the action, nevertheless uses the dominant bloody imagery of the play. This is typical of Shakespeare. The heavens 'threaten' the earth, where man's actions take place, and which Shakespeare typically refers to as a 'stage'. This stage is 'bloody', though. The blood is literal, in the sense that murders have already taken place on the stage (of the theatre), but the evocation of a blood-red stage is powerful. The heavens, disturbed by unnatural acts, produce unnatural darkness in daytime. Shakespeare chooses to mention darkness twice by referring to 'dark night', which 'strangles' the sun. The darkness is murderous, and the metaphor 'lamp' for the sun makes it seem weak by comparison. Night is dominant, the day ashamed, and the enveloping darkness is once again associated with death, through the use of the word 'entomb'. The 'face' of the earth is a very conventional personification, but here the idea of it being entombed suggests a suffocating death. The personification is sharpened by the use of the word 'kiss' in the next line.

Now look at this passage from Act 3 Scene 2.

> Macbeth   Come, seeling night,
> Scarf up the tender eye of pitiful day,
> And with thy bloody and invisible hand
> Cancel and tear to pieces that great bond
> Which keeps me pale! Light thickens, and the crow
> Makes wing to the rooky wood;
> Good things of day begin to droop and drowse;
> While night's black agents to their preys do rouse.

ACTIVITY 4

Answer these questions to show how Shakespeare's choices of language create mood.

1 How many references to darkness are there in the first three lines? You'll have to find out the meaning of 'seeling', and to think about 'scarf up'.

2 What characteristics of day are suggested in the second line?

3 Darkness and blood are persistent images throughout the play. How are the two combined in the third line?

4 What does 'Light thickens' suggest to you? Why is the crow making wing to the rooky wood? Think about colour here.

5 How is a move towards evil suggested in the last two lines? Identify the two references to darkness in the last line.

6 The form underlines the effect of the language here. Rhyme connects things for effect. What things are connected by rhyme here? What is the effect of the repeated sound, do you think? How is the sound of 'drowse' prepared for in the line that it ends?

So far, in this module, form, structure and language have been discussed separately. Often, however, the writer uses these tools together to shape meanings, as in the last two lines of the extract above, and in the extract from *Richard II* on page 50. The rhyming couplets at the end of that scene emphasise the togetherness of Richard and his Queen, and therefore the tragedy of their forced parting, and the language ('dumbly part', 'the rest let sorrow say') further reinforces the hopelessness of the situation. There's another example on page 48 in the speech from *Hamlet*.

Although the tasks you have to do in this module, whether in coursework or examination, will not always demand that you deal with all three, it's a good idea to take the opportunity to do so if you can, to show your knowledge of the range of Shakespeare's skills, and your interpretation of how they work.

AO4: articulate independent opinions and judgements

As stated in the Introduction to this book, it is important to remember that the examiner, if you're doing the exam option, or the marker of your coursework essay, is interested in *your* independent opinion. There isn't a 'correct' interpretation of meaning which they have, and you haven't – it's what *you* think that counts.

Of course, just having an opinion isn't enough. You need to argue your point of view and to support your arguments from the text, showing your '*knowledge and understanding*' (AO2i). It's important, therefore, to plan your answers carefully, sequencing ideas logically and looking to develop them as you write. The examples of coursework tasks given in the following pages should help you to see how you might do this, and you will also see how evidence has to be used.

There are two assessment options for this module: coursework and examination. The basic principle of meeting the Assessment Objectives, which has been shown in the preceding pages, is the same for both options, but there are differences in the sorts of tasks which you might choose.

Coursework option

The specification states that you must study *one* Shakespeare play. For coursework, you can choose any Shakespeare play to study in this module, *except*:

- A play which you might choose in Section A of Module 4 of the Advanced Level course, if you go on to complete it. There are six plays in that section, of which three are by Shakespeare; if you had studied one of these plays as part of AS coursework, you could not then study it as an A Level text.

- A play which you studied at Key Stage 3.

- A play which you studied for GCSE.

In other words, you should not choose any text which you have written about before in an exam, or are likely to at the next level.

You have to write a coursework folder consisting of a single piece of work of about 2,000 words. You will write the piece in school or at home, and then it will be marked by your teacher. Finally, the moderator from the Examination Board will look at your work and all the rest from your centre, and decide on a final mark.

It's very important to select a suitable task for your coursework, one which will enable you to meet the Assessment Objectives for the module. You'll need to keep them very firmly in mind as you plan and write your work. You'll need to work with your teacher in choosing the task, and to seek guidance before you hand in your final draft. Before looking at the sort of task you might choose in this module, and how you might tackle it, here's some advice about the production of coursework which might be useful to you whatever you decide to do.

Producing coursework

There are several things to think about here. Whatever you do, you'll need to think about Assessment Objectives 1 and 2i as you write; but you also need to find a task which deals with the ways in which Shakespeare's '*choices of form, structure and language shape meanings*', (Assessment Objective 3), and which enables you to '*articulate independent opinions and judgements*' (Assessment Objective 4) if you are going to do well. Your task needs to be achievable, too – if you're setting out to write a 2,000-word piece, there's no point in setting yourself a task which can't be done in less than 10,000. As a general rule, the more sharply defined the task is, the better.

You'll probably read the text in class, where you'll have the chance to discuss it with your teacher and other students. But just like preparing your exam texts, you'll need to read it again yourself too. You need to show 'knowledge and understanding' of the text (AO2i) in your writing, and the more you read it the better you will know it, and the more you'll understand it. This will enable you to analyse the text most effectively, and to support your views.

You need to plan your piece of coursework carefully. There are three points to bear in mind here:

1 Spend time on your plan to produce a logical sequence of ideas, which develop an argument and lead to a clear conclusion.

2 Check your plan against the Assessment Objectives – is it clear how and when you are going to achieve them?

3 Because you don't want to have to change your plan much once you start writing, it's worth thinking about length again at this stage. By the time your plan is fleshed out with argument and evidence, does it look as though the word length will be about right? If not, it's worth changing your plan at this stage.

Research may well involve reading articles or essays about your text, from books or the internet, but the most important source of information is still the primary source – the text itself. When you have read secondary sources as part of your research, you must mention them in a bibliography at the end of your essay.

Seven of the thirty marks for this module are for the ability to 'communicate clearly the knowledge, understanding and insight appropriate to literary study, using appropriate terminology and accurate and coherent written expression' (Assessment Objective 1). As long as you give yourself plenty of time to write, you can take more care over the accuracy and clarity of your writing than you can in an exam: you can check it, revise it and improve it when you've finished the first draft. There are specific marks allocated for this, as you can see, so take advantage of them.

Ten marks are available for Assessment Objective 2i – the ability to 'respond with knowledge and understanding to a literary text'. Your understanding will be shown by the quality of your argument; but knowledge has to underpin everything you write, in exams or coursework. In coursework you have the leisure to practise what you have to do under time pressure in the exams, that is, to provide support for what you say from the text. You can demonstrate knowledge by referring to details or echoes of the text, or by quotation. Short quotations (which are usually the most effective) can be included in the body of your writing, while longer quotations can be written on separate lines, so that they're more easily read. If you're quoting lines of verse, you need to indicate the line divisions. Here's an example of all these conventions at work, in some writing about The Winter's Tale:

Before the final moment, Paulina protests twice about the perception that any magic she might perform might be sinful: she refers to 'wicked powers' and 'unlawful business', recalling Prospero's firm 'no' when similarly accused in The Tempest. After the statue moves, Leontes is clear in her defence:

If this be magic, let it be an art
Lawful as eating.

If you're quoting from a secondary source, such as a critic, this should be footnoted, by numbering the quotation and providing the source of the quotation, either at the foot of the page or at the end of the essay.

'How literally should the audience take this moment? Bloom's view is that Paulina, while 'making reasonably clear that she is not a necromancer, is also careful to distance us from realism'.[1]

1. *The Invention of the Human* by Harold Bloom, Fourth Estate, 1999, p. 660.

If you use the words of other writers such as critics in your own writing, you *must* acknowledge them. You have to sign a declaration that the coursework is your own work, and if you 'lift' from other writing without acknowledging it, it is called malpractice, and you may lose all your marks for the module.

When you have completed a first draft of your coursework essay, your teacher may allow you to redraft it, as long as there is enough time to do so. Your teacher is only allowed to give general advice and guidelines as to how you might improve the work, not to correct or rewrite it. Of course, you should heed any advice that you are offered, but basically you should aim for your first draft to be as good as you can make it. It's a lot easier to make minor changes than major ones.

The word limit for AS coursework is 2,000 words. If you exceed it, you may run the risk of being penalised. If your first draft comes to 2,400 words, you can probably cut it fairly easily, and you may want your teacher's guidance about which parts to prune. If it is 4,000 words, though, you're in trouble – cutting sentences here and there, and tightening expression, won't cut it by 50 per cent. This means you have either made a mistake in selecting the task, or at the planning stage, or when you were partway through. Your teacher will give you coursework deadlines, and it's important to stick to them – not just to please your teacher, but to improve your chances of success. You will only be able to cut/redraft/rethink if you've got the time to do it.

Coursework tasks

The list of coursework tasks which follows, and the ways of tackling them, are by no means exhaustive. The tasks simply illustrate some ways of planning and writing successful coursework essays, while keeping the Assessment Objectives firmly in focus. Reading through them may well make you think of tasks you can tackle for your chosen text, or of completely different tasks which access the objectives.

Looking at part of the text

One valuable way of approaching coursework is to analyse a particular passage from the play you're studying, and relate it to the whole play – a technique you'll need to master if you are entering for the exam option. Think about where the passage belongs in the dramatic and thematic structure of the play. How do you think the words and actions reverberate in the rest of the play? What is there in the language of the extract which has significance for the whole play, in your opinion?

As an example of how you might go about a task like this, here's the first scene of *The Tempest*, followed by an activity which could lead to a coursework assignment.

The Tempest Act 1 Scene 1

On a ship at sea. A tempestuous noise of thunder and lightning heard.

[*Enter a* MASTER *and a* BOATSWAIN *severally.*]

MASTER	Boatswain!	
BOATSWAIN	Here, master: what cheer?	
MASTER	Good, speak to the mariners: fall to't, yarely, or we run ourselves aground: bestir, bestir.	

[*Exit.*]

[*Enter* MARINERS.]

BOATSWAIN	Heigh, my hearts! cheerly, cheerly, my hearts! yare, yare! Take in the topsail. Tend to the master's whistle. Blow, till thou burst thy wind, if room enough!	10

[*Enter* ALONSO, SEBASTIAN, ANTONIO, FERDINAND, GONZALO, *and others.*]

ALONSO	Good boatswain, have care. Where's the master? Play the men.	
BOATSWAIN	I pray now, keep below.	
ANTONIO	Where is the master, boatswain?	
BOATSWAIN	Do you not hear him? You mar our labour: keep your cabins: you do assist the storm.	20
GONZALO	Nay, good, be patient.	
BOATSWAIN	When the sea is. Hence! What cares these roarers for the name of king? To cabin: silence! trouble us not.	
GONZALO	Good, yet remember whom thou hast aboard.	
BOATSWAIN	None that I more love than myself. You are a counsellor: if you can command these elements to silence, and work the peace of the present, we will not hand a rope more; use your authority: if you cannot, give thanks you have lived so long, and make yourself ready in your cabin for the mischance of the hour, if it so hap. Cheerly, good hearts! Out of our way, I say.	30

[*Exit.*]

GONZALO   I have great comfort from this fellow: methinks he
           hath no drowning mark upon him; his complexion is
           perfect gallows. Stand fast, good Fate, to his
           hanging! make the rope of his destiny our cable,
           for our own doth little advantage. If he be not
           born to be hanged, our case is miserable.

           [*Exeunt.*]   40

           [*Re-enter* BOATSWAIN.]

BOATSWAIN Down with the topmast! yare! lower, lower! Bring
           her to try with main-course. [*A cry within.*] A plague upon
           this howling! they are louder than the weather, or our office.

           [*Re-enter* SEBASTIAN, ANTONIO, *and* GONZALO.]

           Yet again! what do you here? Shall we give o'er
           and drown? Have you a mind to sink?

SEBASTIAN A pox o' your throat, you bawling, blasphemous,
           incharitable dog!   50

BOATSWAIN Work you then.

ANTONIO   Hang, cur! hang, you whoreson, insolent noisemaker,
           we are less afraid to be drowned than thou art.

GONZALO   I'll warrant him for drowning; though the ship were
           no stronger than a nutshell, and as leaky as an
           unstanched wench.

BOATSWAIN Lay her a-hold, a-hold! Set her two courses; off to
           sea again; lay her off.

           [*Enter* MARINERS, *wet.*]

MARINERS   All lost! to prayers, to prayers! all lost! [*Exeunt.*]   60

BOATSWAIN What, must our mouths be cold?

GONZALO   The king and prince at prayers! let's assist them,
           For our case is as theirs.

SEBASTIAN I am out of patience.

ANTONIO   We are merely cheated of our lives by drunkards:
           This wide-chapp'd rascal – would thou mightst lie drowning,
           The washing of ten tides!

GONZALO   He'll be hang'd yet,
           Though every drop of water swear against it
           And gape at wid'st to glut him.   70

> [*A confused noise within*: 'Mercy on us!' –
> 'We split, we split!' – 'Farewell, my wife and children!' –
> 'Farewell, brother!' – 'We split, we split, we split!']
>
> ANTONIO   Let's all sink wi' the king.
>
> SEBASTIAN   Let's take leave of him.
>
> [*Exeunt* ANTONIO *and* SEBASTIAN.]
>
> GONZALO   Now would I give a thousand furlongs of sea for an acre of barren ground; long heath, brown furze, any thing. The wills above be done! but I would fain die a dry death.   80
>
> [*Exeunt.*]

An interesting way to start thinking about the scene would be to consider which words you would want the audience to hear if you were directing the play. This is a very practical question: in a naturalistic staging of the first scene, it's likely that much of the dialogue would be drowned out by the noise of the thunder and the sea.

ACTIVITY 5

Working alone or in a group, identify which words are most important for the audience to hear and why. As you work, consider the following points:

- **Plot**. What do the audience need to know here that is important to an understanding of events later in the play?

- **Character**. It's unlikely that the audience will make much of individual characters in this scene, but its impact suggests that something will be remembered. Which lines or actions say something significant about the characters? It may not just be about individual characters – you might want to consider how the nobles and the seamen behave towards each other. Do all the noblemen behave in the same way? How do their words and actions foreshadow what we learn of them later?

- **Meanings**. Some words or ideas in the scene are found elsewhere in the play. For instance, Gonzalo's exclamation 'The wills above be done' is not only typical of his attitude and character, but introduces the idea of a controlling power beyond Prospero that is examined many times in the play, for example in Act II: 'Heavens rain grace on that which breeds between 'em'.

- **Language**. The scene is in prose, which is perhaps unsurprising given the frantic, disordered atmosphere which Shakespeare is creating here. There are words, though, which may have echoes elsewhere in the play. For example,

Sebastian remarks 'I'm out of patience' – typical of him, we come to learn, but the word 'patience' takes on a wider significance, particularly in the final scene, as shown in these lines:

ALONSO   Irreparable is the loss, and patience
            Says it is past her cure.

PROSPERO   I rather think
            You have not sought her help; of whose soft grace,
            For the like loss I have her sovereign aid,
            And rest myself content.

The connection between loss, patience and grace made here is not only significant in this play, but in all of Shakespeare's last plays. In Act 5 of *The Winter's Tale*, for instance, exactly the same sequence and type of language is invoked. Look for other examples of language which occur again later in the play.

Working through an exercise like this should provide you with the material to write an essay about Act 1 Scene 1 in relation to the rest of the play, drawing evidence from the passage and elsewhere in the play, as above. You need to show *knowledge* and *understanding* of the play as well as writing about form, structure *and* language. Although the idea for this essay is based on the first scene of the play, it is obvious that you couldn't write an adequate answer without knowledge and understanding of the entire play.

A variation on this approach could be to find a single key line, and show how it reverberates through the play in a number of ways.

ACTIVITY 6

Look at the context of the line 'Are you our daughter?' from *King Lear*, Act 1 Scene 4 and then try to answer the following questions.

FOOL   So out went the candle, and we were left darkling.

LEAR   Are you our daughter?

GONERIL   I would you would make use of your good wisdom . . .

1 Think about the significance of this moment in the plot. What does Lear start to realise, that the audience already knows? Where does this lead?

2 Think about the significance of the question itself. Who is Lear's true daughter? In what sense?

3 The corollary to 'Who are you?' is 'Who am I?' What does this moment start to reveal to Lear about himself?

4 What is happening to Lear's power here? What significance does this have in the context of the whole play? Notice that Goneril's reply is not an answer to the question at all.

5 Lear is questioning what he sees in front of him, with his own eyes, as it were. Perhaps this is the beginning of him being able to 'see straight'. This scene obviously has a huge bearing on one of the central themes of the play, and its associated language, both for Lear's story and the blinding of Gloucester. How is the line 'I stumbled when I saw' (Act 4 Scene 1) relevant to this?

6 The choice of words is interesting, too, especially when compared with Lear's words in Act 4, when he wakes up from madness and recognises Cordelia: 'I think this lady/To be my child Cordelia'. Notice that every word from 'Are you our daughter' has changed: 'our' has become 'my', 'daughter' has become 'child', and so on. Why? What does it tell you about Lear's state of mind, and his change in attitude?

7 'Are you our daughter?' is a half line of verse – the line is incomplete; Goneril's response forms a new line of verse. What happens in the pause created, do you think? Who are the audience looking at? What might Lear be thinking?

If you don't know *King Lear* well you won't have been able to answer all the questions fully, but the Activity will have given you some idea of the scope of features to look for.

ACTIVITY 7

In your chosen play, look for a line which resonates in the text like the one from *King Lear* above, so that you can open up a number of aspects of the play. You should look for a line which is significant in some of these ways:

• form/structure/language

• plot

• character and relationships

• meanings

• action.

Remember that your aim is to write about the line in relation to the rest of the play, showing your *knowledge and understanding*, and that a significant part of this must relate to *form, structure and language*.

Interpreting an aspect of the text

A straightforward way of developing a coursework task would be to look at a particular aspect of the text you're studying and give your reading of it. Once you've started to think about an interpretation, the essential first step is gathering evidence from the text, through a selective re-reading of the text, noting the passages and lines you might use.

Clearly, there are many aspects of your chosen play that you could write about. These could focus on a particular concept in the play and how it is presented. The concept might be peculiar to this play, or it might be one that is found in several of Shakespeare's plays. Some examples are:

- kingship

- justice

- appearance and reality

- time

- fate

- redemption

- the nature of tragedy

- the nature of love.

You could equally choose to look at dramatic features of the text in other ways. Examples might be how the worlds of Rome and Egypt are presented in *Antony and Cleopatra*, how music is used in *Twelfth Night*, or how *The Taming of the Shrew* might be made relevant to a modern audience.

ACTIVITY 8

Choose an aspect of your chosen play to write about, which you think could form the basis of a coursework assignment of 2,000 words. Follow these stages to complete the task.

1 Read the text again selectively, looking for passages relevant to your idea.

2 Make a note of useful evidence (lines from the text) as you work.

3 Review your task in the light of what you've read and found. Will it still work? Is it too slight a task, or too large?

4 Plan your essay, remembering the three things you have to give evidence of to succeed.

5 Write a first draft. Refer to the advice given in the section 'Producing coursework' to help you.

Although the choice might seem very wide when looked at like this, it's vital to remember what you have to show to produce a successful answer. You must deal a) with the ways in which writers' choices of form, structure and language shape meanings, b) you must offer your independent opinion or judgement, and c) you must respond with knowledge and understanding. Part of *knowledge and understanding* which you could lose sight of in this kind of task is the very form of the text you're dealing with. The text is a *play*, and you need to think about how the aspect of the play you have chosen to write about is presented *dramatically*.

Critical analysis of a particular production seen

This might well be a popular choice. After all, the best way to understand the plays as theatre is to see and hear them in the environment for which they were written. You should always seize the chance to see a production of a play you're studying if you can, so why not make it the basis of a coursework assignment?

If this looks like an easy option, think again. You need to do much more than simply describe the production. You must remember that the key Assessment Objectives which you have to address in this module are:

- to show detailed understanding of the ways in which writers' choices of form, structure and language shape meanings

- to articulate informed independent opinions and judgements.

You have to show evidence of these in your writing, so they need to be in your mind when you see the production. You should have a firm idea of what you're looking for (see below), and it is useful to jot some things down immediately after the play – better than writing notes during the play, when there's so much to see and hear. It's even better, of course, if you can see a production twice, to build on what you saw the first time.

To see how this might work, look at this example. A recent production of *Macbeth* had these key features of presentation:

- Lady Macbeth was shown as pregnant. This was clear from her first appearance, and became more pronounced, so that the signs of a miscarriage were evident in the sleepwalking scene.

- The witches were on stage for most of the action, because they played all the parts without names (and Seyton), as well as their own.

Lady Macbeth's pregnancy made her seem even more callous at times. 'I would . . . Have pluck'd my nipple from his boneless gums/And dash'd the brains out' seemed more real and more chilling from a pregnant woman. The blood on her legs in the sleepwalking scene, though horrible, made sense of her suicide and madness. The relationship between the Macbeths achieved an unusual sort of intimacy, and affected the physicality between them. When Macbeth was broken by his wife in Act 1 Scene 7, he fell to his knees and was pulled in to the visibly pregnant stomach on 'We fail?', suggesting a different sort of sexual relationship and control to the one usually chosen.

The witches' presence on stage kept them at the centre of the action, observing and prompting. They became more controlling and omniscient, a part of the action, not separate from it. For instance, the play began with all the male characters on stage, ready for Act 1 Scene 2. The witches (two played by men, one by a woman) were dressed as part of the army, and were picked out by spotlights for the opening lines. They brought down the lights for the interval, too, and for the end of the play: as soldiers again, they were left on stage with Macbeth's head and sword when Malcolm's army departed. The **structure** of the play was altered by the idea for the ending. The play now opened and was ended by the witches, which again emphasised their control.

Lady Macbeth's pregnancy had a bearing on the theme of children in the play. It gave force to Macbeth's concern about the 'barren sceptre' placed in his hand, 'no son of mine succeeding', and his horror at the vision of Banquo's crowned descendants. The vision of the 'bloody child' might have meant Macduff's child – but the tragic culmination of Lady Macbeth's pregnancy produced another meaning.

The greatest effect on the **meaning** of the play came as a result of the presentation of the witches. Because they watched over Macbeth all the time, and prompted him to some extent – throwing the dagger into the stage for him to find, for instance – they seemed to be more in control, and therefore took some of the responsibility for his evil deeds from him. This was particularly clear in Act 5. The decision to play witches as all the unnamed characters meant that Macbeth was surrounded by witches in his castle – everybody else had left, of course. This created more sympathy for Macbeth, perhaps, but also altered the nature of the play.

Writing the assignment

Seeing and hearing these features of the play would have helped you to write a critical analysis of the production, focusing on the appropriate skills. One way to approach *independent opinions and judgements* here would have been to measure the features of the production against your expectations, based on your knowledge of the play. You might have written about what was gained and lost by this interpretation, and whether the play worked dramatically. You might have written about staging elements such as costume and set – but remember, you would have to relate these elements to the interpretation being offered, and your view of the play. You have to address *form, structure and language*, too. You might have done this by providing your view of elements of the play, or by showing how the structure was affected by the interpretation, or how particular words and phrases became important in the production.

Attending a performance

When you attend a performance of a play with a view to writing about it as a piece of coursework, you need to go about it in an organised way if you're going to get the best out of it.

1 Before you go

- You're presumably already familiar with the play, but if you haven't looked at it for a while, remind yourself of it, and think about what you might be expecting to see and hear on the stage.

- Remember that the key Assessment Objectives here are 2i, 3 and 4. What you eventually write will have to relate to these Objectives.

2 At the performance

It's best not to jot things down during the performance – your eyes and ears should be on the stage. If you are going to write anything down, it should be very brief – you can make sense of it afterwards. You could use the interval, if there is one. Here's a list of the sort of things you should be looking for as you watch:

Stage interpretations. Look for any ideas which have informed the production, which suggest how the director and cast want the audience to see the play. Clues to these might be found in:

- the presentation of characters and relationships

- features of language – the way words and lines are spoken, and any particular words or phrases which are made to 'stand out' in some way.

- the way the plot and action are managed – are there any cuts? Changes in sequencing?

- is the set representational? What does it represent or suggest? Does it suggest a particular time period – and does that have a bearing on what the audience think about the action?

- do the costume and props assist the interpretation?

Settings. Looking at the set, costume and props together will reveal something about the setting, and what the production is saying about the play. If the play is set in a different time period from the original performances, this may make the audience think differently about the ideas in the play. This could be reflected not just in the 'dressing' – costume, set, props – but in the way the actors relate to each other in movement and speech.

Your response. In all of this, you need to have your critical faculties alert. How are you responding to what you see? Why?

3 After the performance

Unless you're going to start writing your assignment straight away, now is the time to make some notes, while the performance is still fresh in your mind. Think about the list of points above and anything else that struck you about the production. It's helpful to speak to other people as well at this stage, as they may have seen things that you didn't which might be helpful, or they might have interpreted the production differently. If there are reviews of the production available, read them too, as they may express different interpretations, or different attitudes to the performance.

4 Practising skills

You may not have the luxury of seeing another play before you see the one you're going to write about, but if you do, you could go through this process as a trial run. Or you could apply part of the approach to TV drama or a film version of the play you're studying.

Comparing film and theatre versions

If you have the opportunity to see two productions of a play, this could form an excellent basis for an essay. It's more likely, though, that you might compare a film version to a stage production. With a canvas as large as this, you could choose to narrow the focus of your essay to a particular aspect of the versions. Balancing the two interpretations in the productions, with evidence, and arguing your own view of the play in relation to these two, with evidence showing knowledge and understanding, will meet the requirements of Assessment Objectives 2i and 4. You still need to include *understanding of the ways in which writers' choices of form, structure and language shape meanings*, though, either with evidence from the text or in the way the versions highlight some of these features. Here's how you might go about it.

The process of analysing the stage production would be exactly the same as that suggested above. For the second version you see, though, whether it's stage or screen, part of your observation will be of differences from the first version.

Looking at film is rather different from looking at a stage – particularly if you choose a film version which isn't just a recording of a stage version – and will give you a sharper difference to write about. Here are some ideas for the sort of choices you might make.

- If you were studying *The Tempest*, and had the chance to see a stage production of the play, there are several film versions available on video which you could study alongside the production. The BBC version, with Michael Hordern, offers a fairly conventional reading of the play, with settings quite close to a stage set. At the same time, however, the androgynous representation of Ariel, and the attitudes of Prospero, offer material for discussion of different interpretations. The filming of the opening and the appearances of Ariel and the other spirits would probably be very different from the stage version. Two more unconventional films of the play are directed by Derek Jarman, and Peter Greenaway, whose adaptation has the title *Prospero's Books*. Both treat the play in quite startling ways, and offer much to discuss and write about. An interesting choice might be to look at one of these two films, the BBC version, and a stage production.

- There are several film versions of *Macbeth* available, too. Roman Polanski's film and the recording of the RSC studio production with Ian McKellen and

Judi Dench are quite different, and offer strong interpretations of the relationships between characters. Comparing either or both of these with a stage production would be a viable option.

- The Japanese director Kurosawa's *Ran* is his film version of *King Lear* and would form an excellent basis for a comparison with a stage production – not only in some unusual interpretations, but also for the Japanese setting which the director uses so cleverly to affect the audience's view of the play.

Here are some suggestions for what to look for in a film version of your chosen play.

Watching a film to compare with a play

Much of your attention will be on the same elements as in a stage production (see 'Attending a performance', page 66). Interpretations, and the ways that characters' relationships, setting, costume, etc, develop them, will still be high on your agenda.

There are other elements to look at, though, which are peculiar to film. You need to consider:

1 Use of *setting/place*. Film offers more opportunity than stage, generally speaking, for using a variety of places. Has this been done, and what effect do the settings have on the view of the play being presented?

2 *Lighting/colour*. Because of the nature of the medium, concentration on particular colours, or lighting effects peculiar to cinema, can be used. What do you notice, and why are these colours/effects being used?

3 *Camera distance and angle*. Apart from promenade productions, the angle of the audience member to the stage doesn't alter much, but in film long and short shots, close-ups, panning and tracking shots, and a variety of angles can all be used. The camera techniques that you should look for are those that clearly enhance a particular moment or line in the play. You can then use this in a discussion of **language**.

4 *Cutting/fading*. Film offers a number of techniques for moving from scene to scene, or moment to moment, which are not open to a theatre director. A technique like cut or fade might have been used not simply to speed the action, but to create an effect – perhaps by juxtaposing one moment, event or character sharply against another. Again, it's these motives you should be thinking about once you've identified the technique.

5 *Music/sound*. Of course, music and sound may well be used in the stage production that you see, but music and sound effects are often used more extensively in film. If this is so, what effects do they achieve? Try to be as exact as you can.

---

6 *Special effects*. A play with 'magic' elements, such as *Macbeth*, *The Tempest*, or *A Midsummer Night's Dream* might well be filmed using special effects – and techniques peculiar to film such as split-screen shots could be used in any play. If these techniques have been used, try to work out what the film director's purpose might have been.

7 *Soliloquies*. A feature of most of the Shakespeare plays that you are likely to study is the soliloquy – speeches made by a character when alone on the stage, which enable the audience to see and hear the character's thoughts clearly. Both **form** and **language** are involved here. How have these passages been delivered in the film version?

The danger in writing about a film version of the play(s) you're studying is that you might be tempted to write about the film only as a film. There's no point in writing about any of the techniques above without relating them to **purpose**, that is, the motives of the director in making the audience see the play in a particular way. Remember that it's the play which has to be the centre of your discussion.

Writing the assignment

Because you're focusing on comparing the two versions and the interpretations they offer, your plan should reflect this. You need to give your own view, too, both of the productions and the play. Here are four possible ways of approaching the assignment.

1 • an analysis of version 1

  • an analysis of version 2

  • comparison/contrast of the two versions

  • your view

2 • an analysis of version 1

  • an analysis of version 2, comparing and contrasting as you go

  • your view

3 • an analysis of versions 1 and 2 together, comparing and contrasting features as you go

  • your view

4 • an introduction using your overview, both of text and versions

  • an analysis of versions 1 and 2 together, comparing and contrasting

    features as you go, and using your views as indicators

  • a conclusion, evaluating the comparative success of the versions.

Any of these approaches could succeed. Remember that in writing the essay you will need to show knowledge as well as understanding, by using details not only from the productions but from the text(s) themselves.

Proposals for staging the text

This is an attractive option, in that it will allow you to think about the play both practically and creatively. There are some dangers, though. There would be no point in writing simply about costume, setting, stage action, or any other feature of staging without relating them to your interpretation of the play – your *informed independent judgement*. You must show *knowledge and understanding*, too, so your suggestions need to be referenced in the text, and you must address some features of *form, structure and language*.

Another danger is writing too much. You should not try to write a full production script, working through the play chronologically: the outcome would inevitably be long and repetitive. It's the principles of staging your interpretation that you're concerned with – the different production elements should be seen in this light. You'll probably want to consider some key scenes or moments from the play, so that you can focus on particular features of form or language.

In the third suggestion for a coursework task, on page 64 above, the example of a production of *Macbeth* featured a particular interpretation of the witches. If you had come up with this idea, you can see that your interpretation would have necessitated the following staging elements:

- How they were dressed – they would have to be in a variety of costumes to suit the parts they played, such as soldiers, waiting gentlewomen, and so on.

- The gender of the players – in this production, there was only one female witch, and two males, one white and one black. This in itself offered a variety of role playing.

- How they behaved – their degree of control was indicated by the way they seemed to command the lighting, and the throwing of the dagger into the stage for Macbeth to find.

- The management of the action – this would be very noticeable to the audience, as they closed both halves of the play.

- The effects on stage of their presentation. It was mentioned that in Act 5 they surrounded Macbeth, and stage positioning would emphasise this. This in its turn, together with the other elements above, would suggest an interpretation of Macbeth – that his responsibility for his evil deeds was lessened by their evident control.

ACTIVITY 9

Using your text, think about how you would like to present the play, looking at the range of staging elements listed below and taking into account the play and what you want to do with it.

1 The colour of costumes might be significant, to suggest character, or what the character represents. Obviously period might be significant, too: different settings, which might suggest an interpretation of the text, could be suggested by costume, probably in conjunction with set and props.

2 Male characters don't necessarily have to be played by men, or women by women. Shakespeare's women were played by boys, of course, and in recent times several leading male parts have been played by women, with particular effects: Fiona Shaw played Richard II, for instance, and Kathryn Hunter played King Lear.

3 How the character is 'played', in terms of how the actors behave, speak the lines, and what they choose to emphasise, might be really significant and useful in enabling you to write about language. But remember that whatever you say needs to be linked to your intentions, to what the interpretation is. You might want to suggest that particular words or phrases are picked out by the actor(s), because of the interpretation you're suggesting.

4 In the same way, it will only be valuable to comment on stage action and stage positioning, if you can link it successfully to interpretation – and it's how the audience sees it that's important.

5 It's a good idea to show these staging elements, or some of them, working at particular moments in a scene or part of a scene where this staging and interpretation will be particularly clear.

Writing the assignment

It's important to frame your staging suggestions in the light of the relevant Assessment Objectives. This begins at the thinking stage, and continues with planning. You need to show *knowledge and understanding*, of course, so your suggestions should include quotes from the text, and show a considered and supported view of what it might mean. Your *independent opinion and judgement* will be shown by your interpretation of the play, and you must seek to include some *detailed understanding of the ways writers' choices of form, structure and language shape meanings* in your explanation of your staging suggestions, and in your views on the play as a whole.

Examination option

If you choose the examination option, you will have a choice of three Shakespeare plays and, as this is an open book module, you will be able to take your text into the examination room with you. This means that the questions will probably focus on one part of the text, perhaps a scene or a number of lines, and ask you to look at them again and write about them. You may be asked to write about these lines in relation to the rest of the play, or just about the lines, though in doing so you'll have to draw on your knowledge and understanding of the rest of the play if you're to do well. Some examples of the sort of tasks you might face, and how to think about them, are given below, but the skills required in approaching the text are the same as those you've worked on throughout this section.

Looking at a single scene

You might be asked to look at a single scene in the play, and comment on some of its features. You could be asked how you might direct it, too; 'Proposals for staging the text' on page 70 suggests how you might tackle such a task. The sort of features you could be asked about are likely to include details of form, structure and language, presentation of characters and relationships, dramatic effects or functions, and how some of the writer's meanings might appear here. You can see that these relate to Assessment Objectives 2i and 3. Key words like 'how appropriate', 'how would you', and 'consider' will remind you that you have to deal with Assessment Objective 4, too, and offer your *independent opinion and judgement*.

Here are the first 18 lines from *Antony and Cleopatra*. You could be asked to read Act 1 Scene 1 and consider its dramatic effect, and the presentation of the characters of Antony and Cleopatra.

> [*Enter* DEMETRIUS *and* PHILO.]
>
> PHILO   Nay, but this dotage of our general's
> O'erflows the measure; those his goodly eyes,
> That o'er the files and musters of the war
> Have glow'd like plated Mars, now bend, now turn,
> The office and devotion of their view
> Upon a tawny front; his captain's heart,
> Which in the scuffles of great fights hath burst
> The buckles on his breast, reneges all temper,
> And is become the bellows and the fan
> To cool a gipsy's lust. Look! where they come: 10
>
> [*Flourish. Enter* ANTONY, CLEOPATRA, *her Ladies, the Train, with Eunuchs fanning her.*]
>
> Take but good note, and you shall see in him
> The triple pillar of the world transform'd
> Into a strumpet's fool; behold and see.
>
> CLEOPATRA   If it be love indeed, tell me how much.
>
> MARK ANTONY   There's beggary in the love that can be reckon'd.
>
> CLEOPATRA   I'll set a bourn how far to be belov'd.
>
> MARK ANTONY   Then must thou needs find out new heaven, new earth.
>
> [*Enter an* ATTENDANT.]
>
> ATTENDANT   News, my good lord, from Rome.
>
> MARK ANTONY   Grates me; the sum.

Form, structure, language

The first point here is **structural**. This is the opening of the play, and (typically) the audience are given a view of the central characters before they enter, creating expectation, and giving a context for the appearance, albeit from a Roman point of view. The scene is structured to begin and end with comments from the minor characters before Antony and Cleopatra appear and after they leave; and the whole play ends with comments about them, again from a Roman.

Although this might suggest a Chorus-like function for these characters, the audience are left in no doubt that they are not impartial. They enter in the middle of a conversation, marked by 'Nay, but', and Philo's **language** shows his allegiance to Antony: he is referred to as 'our' general in the first line, and Cleopatra is a 'gipsy' to him. His words are full of military detail: 'files', 'musters', 'plated Mars', 'great fights', 'buckles'. Change is signalled by 'bend' and 'turn', underlined by the form: the repetition of 'now bend, now turn' enables the stresses to fall on the words showing change, and lifts them out for notice. The change is away from 'goodly', though, and is characterised as 'dotage' which 'O'erflows the measure', the first mentions of age and excess, key ideas in the play. Duty is another concept at the heart of the moral discussion, and is also introduced here: Antony's 'office and devotion' have strayed to sensuality. The last words before Cleopatra's entrance are pejorative: 'a gipsy's lust', and 'transform'd into a strumpet's fool' follows close behind.

The language of the two central characters initially upholds Philo's view. Despite the grand entrance, their talk is clearly private, and concerns only themselves, i.e. the extent of their love. Their importance, and the sense of something universal beyond them, is nevertheless being signalled by language already: Philo refers to Antony as 'the triple pillar of the world', and finding out 'new heaven, new earth' suggests, through hyperbole, the extent of their passion. Antony's mind is clearly not on his military duty: 'Grates me; the sum' is not only sharp and truncated, but is also emphasised as such by completing the messenger's line. **Form** and **language** work together here.

Dramatic effects

As this is the opening of the play, the audience might expect a dramatic flourish of some sort, in action or words, instead of which they are privy to a conversation which has already begun. The entrance is held back, perhaps making the audience, like Demetrius, anticipate it even more. When it does come, Philo signals its significance and the importance of observing very strongly: 'Look . . . Take but good note . . . you shall see . . . behold and see.' This forms a strong dramatic context for Antony and Cleopatra's opening words. The words are not regal, though, again denying some expectations, perhaps, but are private, bearing out Philo's view of Antony's obsession. His sharpness to the Messenger is dramatic, too: This rudeness does not become Antony as a leader (though we see it several times in the play as characteristic of Cleopatra), and it indicates his dereliction of duty.

You can see that in dealing with just these 18 lines it's possible to examine form, structure and language, presentation of characters and relationships, dramatic effects and functions, and how some of the writer's meanings emerge. In the exam you would probably be asked to look at a longer passage than this. If you'd gone on to look at the whole scene, you might have mentioned Cleopatra's response, which is against expectations, and sharp, shown by her language: 'Nay, and most like', beginning her presentation as either a 'wrangling Queen' or of 'infinite variety'. Antony's language is heightened and noble, while indicating the enormity of his treachery to Rome's ideals: 'Let Rome in Tiber melt'. The idea of falling is present, too, and that of punishment for these attitudes. Antony's diction is full of the values represented by Egypt in the play: 'the love of Love', 'her soft hours', 'pleasure', 'sport'. 'Speak not to us' is a dramatic and dismissive exit line, leaving Roman disapproval centre stage again, with a sense of a declined and changed leader who is 'not Antony' – a failed ideal.

Now read this next extract from the same play and work through Activity 10 that follows.

CLEOPATRA	O sun!
	Burn the great sphere thou mov'st in, darkling stand
	The varying shore o' the world. O Antony,
	Antony, Antony! Help, Charmian, help, Iras, help;
	Help, friends below; let's draw him hither.
MARK ANTONY	Peace!
	Not Caesar's valour hath o'erthrown Antony,
	But Antony's hath triumph'd on itself.
CLEOPATRA	So it should be, that none but Antony
	Should conquer Antony; but woe 'tis so!
MARK ANTONY	I am dying, Egypt, dying; only
	I here importune death awhile, until
	Of many thousand kisses the poor last
	I lay upon thy lips.
CLEOPATRA	I dare not, dear, –
	Dear my lord, pardon – I dare not,
	Lest I be taken: not the imperious show
	Of the full-fortun'd Caesar ever shall
	Be brooch'd with me; if knife, drugs, serpents, have
	Edge, sting, or operation, I am safe:
	Your wife Octavia, with her modest eyes
	And still conclusion, shall acquire no honour
	Demuring upon me. But come, come, Antony, –
	Help me, my women, – we must draw thee up.
	Assist, good friends.

MARK ANTONY	O, quick, or I am gone.
CLEOPATRA	Here's sport indeed! How heavy weighs my lord!
	Our strength is all gone into heaviness,
	That makes the weight. Had I great Juno's power,
	The strong-wing'd Mercury should fetch thee up,
	And set thee by Jove's side. Yet come a little,
	Wishers were ever fools. O! come, come, come;

[*They heave* MARK ANTONY *aloft to* CLEOPATRA.]

	And welcome, welcome! die where thou hast liv'd:
	Quicken with kissing; had my lips that power,
	Thus would I wear them out.
ALL	A heavy sight!
MARK ANTONY	I am dying, Egypt, dying:
	Give me some wine, and let me speak a little.

ACTIVITY 10

This passage is taken from Act 4 Scene 15, of *Antony and Cleopatra*, when the dying Antony is brought to the monument where Cleopatra has locked herself away from Caesar. Look for features of form, structure and language, including the way that characters are presented, dramatic effects, and the central ideas of the play, using the following questions to help you.

1 Look at the first two lines. How is the sense of the lovers being of huge significance, and their love transcending the ordinary, presented here? Look at the effects of all of the words here, not just one. Are there any other references to huge powers in the passage?

2 One of the language features in this passage is repetition. Look for all the repetitions. In Cleopatra's first speech, the repetitions increase the sense of urgency. How does the rhythm of the lines highlight this urgency?

3 Urgency is communicated by form in another way here. Look for instances where one character's speech ends with a half line of verse and another character cuts in and completes this line with the beginning of their speech.

4 There's also a pause created by an incomplete line. When Antony repeats 'I am dying, Egypt, dying' at the end of this extract, the line is not completed. What is the effect of this?

5 Cleopatra's language is still full of playfulness and sensuality. Even at this moment, she uses the word 'sport', reminding the audience of her 'sports' with Antony during the course of the play – which have led to this situation. How might 'heavy' and 'weight' refer to their sexual relations? (Remember Cleopatra's reference to Antony's horse: 'O happy horse, to bear the weight

of Antony!' Act 1 Scene 5.) Think about the sexual ambiguity of 'come' (repeated), and 'die' linked with 'quicken'. Use a dictionary if necessary. 'Lips' and 'wine' are still at the forefront of their minds, too.

6 Whose fault is Antony's death, according to both characters?

7 Although Antony and Cleopatra are a couple, as the title suggests, they are self-obsessed as well, as seen in their failure to respond to the call of duty to anything beyond themselves. Look carefully at the words of both characters here, and decide whether they are really interested in each other, or simply in themselves. Notice, for instance, that Antony doesn't ask Cleopatra to kiss him; he states rather patronisingly that he will kiss her, 'I lay upon thy lips'.

8 Clearly the raising up of Antony to the monument is a dramatic moment. How does Shakespeare keep the audience waiting for him to be raised, and for their moment of reunion, thereby creating suspense?

Looking at a scene in the context of the whole play

Some of the ideas which may be useful to you in considering how to tackle this sort of task are dealt with in 'Looking at part of the text', in the coursework suggestions on page 57. An exam question might ask you to see the scene in relation to the rest of the play in some way, showing how details relate to descriptions elsewhere, or the significance of this particular scene. The examples below only deal with relatively short extracts, compared to what you might be asked to look at in the exam. The passages are used to show you the sort of things you need to be thinking about. You'll always be asked to discuss form, structure and language, dramatic features, and the writer's meanings, so the focus in here, in the examples below, will be on the skill of making comparisons with the rest of the play.

Here are the opening lines of *Twelfth Night*:

[*Enter* DUKE ORSINO, CURIO, *and other Lords; Musicians attending.*]

DUKE ORSINO   If music be the food of love, play on;
Give me excess of it, that, surfeiting,
The appetite may sicken, and so die.
That strain again! it had a dying fall:
O! it came o'er my ear like the sweet sound,
That breathes upon a bank of violets,
Stealing and giving odour. Enough! no more:
'Tis not so sweet now as it was before.
O spirit of love! how quick and fresh art thou,
That, notwithstanding thy capacity   10
Receiveth as the sea, nought enters there,

	Of what validity and pitch soe'er,
	But falls into abatement and low price,
	Even in a minute: so full of shapes is fancy
	That it alone is high fantastical.
CURIO	Will you go hunt, my lord?
DUKE ORSINO	What, Curio?
CURIO	The hart.
DUKE ORSINO	Why, so I do, the noblest that I have:
	O! when mine eyes did see Olivia first,
	Methought she purg'd the air of pestilence!

20

It's clear that a director may well choose to open the play with the musicians playing, in order to support Orsino's first line. As well as providing a dramatically pleasing opening, it would also be appropriate: music and song pervade the play, and structurally it would frame the action of the play with music, as the Clown's song ends it. Even if this choice isn't made, 'music' is the second word of the play, and it is referred to as having a 'dying fall'. Again, this connects with the mood of the final song, but also with several of the songs in between, and perhaps with the whole flavour of the ending, which can be played very darkly. Even in these few lines, the sweetness disappears, according to the changeable Orsino.

Love is signalled in the first line too, and it is an exploration of love that is at the heart of the play, in all its variations: sibling love, heterosexual love, homosexual love, the love of friends, self-love. Orsino's love is unbalanced and excessive, and not based on a realistic foundation; he pleads to lose his love by being sick. He cannot break his obsessive thoughts; when Curio suggests hunting 'the hart', he turns the thought back to his own suffering at the hands of love. Much is made of the image of eyes in the play, both what they see and how they see. Orsino's obsession starts from the moment 'when mine eyes did see Olivia first' – and a similar thing happens to Olivia herself later. Here, after the hearing sense is appealed to by music, it is taste which is invoked. Food and 'appetite' are important in the play too, not only in the name and habits of Sir Toby Belch, but as metaphors for a love of life: 'Dost thou think, because thou art virtuous, there shall be no more cakes and ale?' Orsino, typically, uses an image which takes eating to excess. To complete the sensual theme in Orsino's lyrical language, the smell of violets is invoked too.

Here the 'spirit of love' is seen as quickly changing by Orsino, and then is seen again later in Olivia's sudden switch of attention away from her dead brother to the disguised Viola, and in Orsino's own swift change from Olivia to Viola. This is in contrast to the spirit suggested by Viola herself of 'Patience on a monument'. 'Fancy' might well describe the nature of Orsino's love. Shakespeare portrays the sea as a leveller, and it is the action of the sea in the shipwreck which changes the situation, by releasing Viola into Orsino's court, and changes the situation again when her brother arrives, and finally precipitates the ending when the sea-captain reappears.

Although this analysis has concentrated on linking this passage to the rest of the play, you should notice that the focus is on the same features dealt with in the first example of an exam question: form, structure and language, the presentation of character and ideas, and dramatic features.

Now study this passage from the ending of the same play (Act 5 Scene 1) and work through Activity 11.

OLIVIA	Alas, poor fool, how have they baffled thee!
CLOWN	Why, 'some are born great, some achieve greatness, and some have greatness thrown upon them.' I was one, sir, in this interlude; one Sir Topas, sir; but that's all one. 'By the Lord, fool, I am not mad.' But do you remember? 'Madam, why laugh you at such a barren rascal? an you smile not, he's gagged:' and thus the whirligig of time brings in his revenges.
MALVOLIO	I'll be revenged on the whole pack of you.
	[*Exit.*]
OLIVIA	He hath been most notoriously abus'd. 10
DUKE ORSINO	Pursue him and entreat him to a peace; He hath not told us of the captain yet: When that is known and golden time convents, A solemn combination shall be made Of our dear souls. Meantime, sweet sister, We will not part from hence. Cesario, come; For so you shall be, while you are a man; But when in other habits you are seen, Orsino's mistress and his fancy's queen.
	[*Exeunt all, except* CLOWN.]
CLOWN	[*Sings.*]
	When that I was and a little tiny boy, 20 With hey, ho, the wind and the rain, A foolish thing was but a toy, For the rain it raineth every day . . .

ACTIVITY 11

Responding to the questions below will help you to see how you could relate this passage to the rest of the play.

1 As this is the end of the play, the audience are deliberately reminded of earlier moments in the play. For instance, 'some are born great, some achieve greatness,/and some have greatness thrust upon them' is from the letter which forms the basis of the plot against Malvolio. Try to find other references or echoes which remind you either directly or indirectly of other moments in the play.

2 Time is an important element in the play, particularly in the words of Feste, the clown. If you haven't done so already in answering the first question, remind yourself of the theme of time in Feste's songs. Now look at his two mentions of time here. What does time bring? Consider the effect of this on the mood of the ending.

3 'Golden time' suggests a rich moment, in line with the successful romantic outcome for four of the characters. How is this feeling undermined by what happens on stage immediately before and after Orsino's speech?

4 Orsino refers to Viola's disguise. Who else has been disguised in the play? What is the effect of these disguises? Orsino wants to see Viola now in 'other habits'. How does the way people are dressed in the play affect the action and outcome?

5 The reference to 'his fancy's queen' should make you think of the first scene, above, and the nature of Orsino's 'fancy'.

6 Think about the dramatic nature of the stage action here. Malvolio exits, vowing revenge – hardly a conventional feature in the ending of a comedy. Although Olivia pities him – think of her earlier attitudes – Orsino orders that he be pursued, but the 'peace' is not seen on stage. What difference does this make?

7 The recognition and reconciliation immediately before this passage, and perhaps the expectation by the audience that this will be the mood of the ending, suggest that 'golden time' will unite all. Malvolio exits alone, though. Who else is not part of this unity at the end, and why?

8 Feste's song ends the play. How does the rest of the play lead to this moment? You need to think about:

- the beginning of the play

- the songs in the play

- Feste's attitude to love and time

- the universality of the words of Feste's song

- the effect of having a character on the stage alone at the final moment.

Focusing on these points should enable you to explain your ideas about the ending of the play.

Comparing two extracts

Another possible style of question is a comparison of two shorter passages, perhaps asking you to look at change or development between the two. Form/structure/language, dramatic effects, and independent opinion and judgement still need to be dealt with, however.

Here's an example of how this sort of task might be approached, using two passages from *The Taming of the Shrew*, the first from Act 3 Scene 2 and the second from Act 5 Scene 2.

PASSAGE 1

KATHARINA	Nay, then,
	Do what thou canst, I will not go to-day;
	No, nor to-morrow, nor till I please myself.
	The door is open, sir, there lies your way;
	You may be jogging whiles your boots are green;
	For me, I'll not be gone till I please myself.
	'Tis like you'll prove a jolly surly groom,
	That take it on you at the first so roundly.
PETRUCHIO	O Kate! content thee: prithee, be not angry.
KATHARINA	I will be angry: what hast thou to do? 10
	Father, be quiet; he shall stay my leisure.
GRUMIO	Ay, marry, sir, now it begins to work.
KATHARINA	Gentlemen, forward to the bridal dinner:
	I see a woman may be made a fool,
	If she had not a spirit to resist.
PETRUCHIO	They shall go forward, Kate, at thy command.
	Obey the bride, you that attend on her;
	Go to the feast, revel and domineer,
	Carouse full measure to her maidenhead,
	Be mad and merry, or go hang yourselves: 20
	But for my bonny Kate, she must with me.
	Nay, look not big, nor stamp, nor stare, nor fret;
	I will be master of what is mine own:
	She is my goods, my chattels; she is my house,
	My household stuff, my field, my barn,
	My horse, my ox, my ass, my anything;
	And here she stands, touch her whoever dare;
	I'll bring mine action on the proudest he
	That stops my way in Padua. Grumio,
	Draw forth thy weapon, we are beset with thieves; 30
	Rescue thy mistress, if thou be a man.
	Fear not, sweet wench, they shall not touch thee, Kate:
	I'll buckler thee against a million.

[*Exeunt* PETRUCHIO, KATHARINA, *and* GRUMIO.]

The task is to consider the alterations in Kate's feelings, and in the relationship between the two central characters, and to consider the dramatic effects of the two passages.

You would begin, probably, by looking carefully at the first passage. There are several **language** features in Kate's speeches here which present her feelings. From 'Nay then' her words are full of negatives – what she will not do. There are six examples in the first eight lines. The syntax is simple and direct, as in 'For me, I'll not be gone till I please myself', and this is reinforced by form: she has twelve lines here, and eight of them are end-stopped, making her speech very blunt and clear. Of the eight sentences, five are statements (though 'there lies your way' makes one of them nearly a command), two are commands, to her father and the 'Gentlemen', and one is a rhetorical question. There is no doubt here. She has little time for men: 'groom', father, gentlemen are to be dismissed and commanded, and 'a woman' must have 'a spirit to resist'. Her husband, certainly, cannot command her: 'What hast thou to do?'

Petruchio, typically and cleverly, turns Kate's words against her. He pretends to agree with her, and commands 'Obey the bride', before inventing an imaginary protest from the company. His language is as plain and strong as hers – 'I will be', 'she is' – and even more commanding. There are eight commands in his speech at the end of the extract, and again form underlines the decisiveness: in 'I will be' and 'She is' the stress falls on the second syllable, and in the imperative 'she must with me' it is the modal verb and the pronoun that are stressed. Lists are used twice to emphasise determination and ownership. 'Big', 'stamp', 'stare', and 'fret' are all emphasised by the rhythm, as are the items in the last of things which Kate is, according to Petruchio. 'Thing' is the last item, in fact, perhaps chosen to stress not only ownership, already insisted on by the repetition nine times of 'my', but also the equating of Kate to inanimate objects as well as beasts. The list carries biblical echoes, too, perhaps to suggest further the patriarchal attitude. Kate has not yet learnt to conform, so she must be taught a lesson.

Dramatically, the seizure of Kate and her removal, presumably forcibly, are not only strong in terms of stage action, but also symbolise Petruchio's control and ownership of her, achieved by physical force. The dramatic centre of the passage, though, is when Petruchio starts to speak at 'They shall go forward', where the conflict between them is addressed directly. It is noticeable that Kate does not speak again before she is removed – perhaps she is prevented from doing so?

Now look at the second passage, and start to look for differences. Working through Activity 12 that follows should help you to explore the contrasts in detail.

PASSAGE 2

KATHARINA

Fie, fie! unknit that threatening unkind brow,
And dart not scornful glances from those eyes,
To wound thy lord, thy king, thy governor:
It blots thy beauty as frosts do bite the meads,
Confounds thy fame as whirlwinds shake fair buds,
And in no sense is meet or amiable.
A woman mov'd is like a fountain troubled,
Muddy, ill-seeming, thick, bereft of beauty;
And while it is so, none so dry or thirsty
Will deign to sip or touch one drop of it.
Thy husband is thy lord, thy life, thy keeper,
Thy head, thy sovereign; one that cares for thee,
And for thy maintenance commits his body
To painful labour both by sea and land,
To watch the night in storms, the day in cold,
Whilst thou liest warm at home, secure and safe;
And craves no other tribute at thy hands
But love, fair looks and true obedience;
Too little payment for so great a debt.
Such duty as the subject owes the prince,
Even such a woman oweth to her husband;
And when she is froward, peevish, sullen, sour,
And not obedient to his honest will,
What is she but a foul contending rebel,
And graceless traitor to her loving lord? –
I am asham'd that women are so simple
To offer war where they should kneel for peace,
Or seek for rule, supremacy, and sway,
When they are bound to serve, love, and obey.
Why are our bodies soft, and weak, and smooth,
Unapt to toil and trouble in the world,
But that our soft conditions and our hearts
Should well agree with our external parts?
Come, come, you froward and unable worms!
My mind hath been as big as one of yours,
My heart as great, my reason haply more,
To bandy word for word and frown for frown;
But now I see our lances are but straws,
Our strength as weak, our weakness past compare,
That seeming to be most which we indeed least are.
Then vail your stomachs, for it is no boot,
And place your hands below your husband's foot:
In token of which duty, if he please,
My hand is ready; may it do him ease.

PETRUCHIO

Why, there's a wench! Come on, and kiss me, Kate.

LUCENTIO

Well, go thy ways, old lad, for thou shalt ha't.

VINCENTO	'Tis a good hearing when children are toward.
LUCENTIO	But a harsh hearing when women are froward.
PETRUCHIO	Come, Kate, we'll to bed.
	We three are married, but you two are sped . . .

ACTIVITY 12

1 Kate's language is quite different here. Look carefully at the length and complexity of the sentences, and the number of end-stopped lines. Look at statements, commands and questions too, and notice who is being commanded, in contrast to the first passage. Notice the structures she uses, which build item after item in a very controlled, almost formal way. Look back to the first passage again, to find a clear contrast to use as evidence.

2 There are no rhyming couplets in the first passage. Check this second passage for rhymes, and their frequency. Why should there be rhymes here, and not in the first?

3 Kate's attitude to men, and to husbands, seems to have changed completely. What do the lists beginning 'thy lord' remind you of in the first passage – and who was speaking then? What might this linguistic choice be suggesting about the change in Kate?

4 Look through the speech for all the words referring to men. Notice how many of them suggest ruling.

5 Some of Kate's language suggests war being waged by women, where 'they should kneel for peace'. Find these words, and consider what they imply about men, and about women.

6 Look at what Kate suggests about the nature of women, and the various ways in which she suggests that they are weak.

7 Kate's closing words form a dramatic gesture. Silence is also dramatic, though. Petruchio says very little here, compared to his volubility in the rest of the play. What is the significance of this?

8 There are a number of ways you might interpret Kate's apparent capitulation to Petruchio, which is certainly uncomfortable for a modern audience. Perhaps she is being ironic throughout, even to the extent of using Petruchio's linguistic terms and structures. Do the men really have the power here? Nevertheless, Petruchio seems to be the winner in several senses. Your response to the ending, which the comparison invites you to make, will clearly enable you to form an *independent opinion and judgement*, informed by *knowledge and understanding*, and taking into account the ways in which Shakespeare's uses of *form, structure and language shape meanings*. In other words, you can address all the relevant Assessment Objectives.

The suggestions and activities given in this exam option section are not meant to be exhaustive. They are examples of the sort of tasks you might be set, and the ways in which you must pay attention to the Assessment Objectives in responding to them.

Module **3** Texts in Context – Drama and Poetry

This module carries 40% of the total marks for the AS level course.
The marks are divided amongst the Assessment Objectives like this:

ASSESSMENT OBJECTIVES

AO1 communicate clearly the knowledge, understanding and insight appropriate to literary study, using appropriate terminology and accurate and coherent written expression
(5% of the final AS mark; 2.5% of the final A level mark)

AO2i respond with knowledge and understanding to literary texts of different types and periods
(5% of the final AS mark; 2.5% of the final A level mark)

AO3 show detailed understanding of the ways in which writers' choices of form, structure and language shape meanings
(5% of the final AS mark; 2.5% of the final A level mark)

AO4 articulate independent opinions and judgements informed by different interpretations of literary texts by other readers
(10% of the final AS mark; 5% of the final A level mark)

AO5i show understanding of the contexts in which literary texts are written and understood.
(15% of the final AS mark; 7.5% of the final A level mark)

All the Assessment Objectives are tested in this module, and they are allocated to period in the following way:

Pre 1900 Drama and Poetry
Assessment Objective 1
Assessment Objective 2i – split between both sections
Assessment Objective 3
Assessment Objective 5i – the dominant objective worth 15% of the marks

Post 1900 Drama and Poetry
Assessment Objective 1
Assessment Objective 2i – split between both sections
Assessment Objective 3
Assessment Objective 4 – the dominant objective worth 10% of the marks

The main emphasis for your studies will be the dominant Assessment Objective for each period, although it is necessary to pay attention to the other objectives as well.

Content

This module meets the syllabus requirements for drama and poetry. It also meets the Pre 1900 period requirement.

The structure of the module

Module 3 is spit into two sections: Section A Drama and Section B Poetry. Each section is then sub-divided by period into Pre 1900 and Post 1900.

The examination

The question paper is split into two sections, Section A Drama, and Section B Poetry. You will answer one question from each genre, remembering that the two texts *must* be from different periods. You are allowed to take your text into the examination.

3 Section A: Drama

Assessment Objectives 1 and 2i will be automatically met as you work through your texts and acquire knowledge, understanding and critical terminology. Assessment Objective 3 will be considered side-by-side with your study of contexts, as you will demonstrate how the various contexts are conveyed through the writers' choices of form, structure and language.

Understanding contexts

This is the *only time* that you will be tested on Assessment Objective 5i at AS level, but there is no need to feel concerned about this objective. In the Introduction you looked at the various types of contexts you need to consider:

- *the context of a period or era, including significant social, historical, political and cultural processes*: you will see that this context will involve the consideration of themes in a way that is familiar from your studies at GCSE.

- *the context of a given or specific passage in terms of the whole work from which it is taken*: this is a part-to-whole context where you would be expected to relate an extract to the whole text.

- *the context of the work in terms of other texts, including other works by the same author*: this will apply to the poetry section where you will consider several poems by the same author.

- *the literary context, including the question of generic factors and period-specific styles*. A **genre** is a specific kind of writing. At AS level you will look at three different genres, the novel, drama and poetry, exploring the particular characteristics of each type.

What are contexts?

It might be helpful to think about **contexts** as two sets of frameworks, the outer and the inner frames or contexts related to each text.

A writer may develop a *social context* within the text where there is exploration of aspects of society such as love or marriage, faith or social behaviour and morality. The inner context or frame could also be *political*, with enquiries into political behaviour, or *legal*, with the exploration of matters such as justice. *Historical contexts* could involve issues such as slavery or governmental attitudes. You will soon find that within the frame of reference which the author constructs you are back to the familiar territory of exploring themes or concerns.

The outer contexts would include matters of *genre*, such as the relationship of a Jacobean play to the revenge genre, or of *period*, such as how historical or stylistic matters have affected a particular author.

At AS level the contexts may generally be drawn from within the text itself. Any explanation necessary to 'place' your chosen text in a context external to the text may be given by your teacher, or will be explained in this book. At A2 level you will be expected to explore these outer contexts yourself and relate them to the text.

Pre 1900 Drama

The aim of this section is to explore a series of contexts drawn from several plays. You will learn how to compile evidence from a text in order to demonstrate how a particular context becomes evident and acquires significance for your interpretation of the play.

How to explore contexts

Although this section may look at only one or two contexts from a particular text, this does *not* mean that it is the *only* context evident in that text. This section offers a demonstration of how to explore a particular context as an example of how you should investigate contexts generally. Likewise, do not think that any reading of a play discussed here is the sole reading. Remember that all texts are open to several different readings.

Here are the different types of contexts which will be used as examples of how to cover Assessment Objective 5i:

- contexts of period and genre in the morality play

- the dramatic context of the Renaissance tragic hero

- the theatrical context

- moral contexts

- the biographical context

- the context of love and of family relationships.

The pre 1900 drama in this module is drawn from three main periods or types: Elizabethan, Restoration and the Comedy of Manners.

Elizabethan drama – *Dr Faustus* by Christopher Marlowe

AO5i: The two **contexts** to be explored are:

1 *Dr Faustus* as a **morality play**: the contexts of period and of genre.

2 Faustus himself in the context of the **Elizabethan tragic hero,** which involves the contexts of period and genre.

Remember that there are other readings possible within these contexts, and that there are other readings of the text overall. For the purposes of this example, we will consider a Christian reading, but this is not the only interpretation of this play.

AO2i: knowledge and understanding of the text

In *Dr Faustus* Marlowe may, in one interpretation, be seen to explore the Elizabethan celebration of the achievement of Renaissance man. But at the same time he explores the darker aspects of Faustus's pride, which leads to sin and damnation.

In the play, Faustus makes a pact with the devil: he will surrender his soul on a set date in exchange for skills in the magic art of necromancy. Necromancy is the art of predicting the future by means of communication with the dead, a sort of black magic. In Christian terms, knowledge of the future belongs only to God. So, in one interpretation of the play, Faustus may be seen as wrong in trying to assume this power. He comes to regret his pact with the devil, but despair affects his ability to repent.

AO3/AO5i: how the writer expresses the ideas related to these contexts

---

Dr Faustus as a morality play: the contexts of period and of genre

The **morality play** was one of the popular types of drama in the fourteenth and fifteenth centuries. The subject of the plays was man, how he survived temptation and overcame his sins or errors to achieve salvation. There were at least two plays which were significant for later drama and for *Dr Faustus* – *The Castle of Perseverance* and *Everyman*.

A. **Castle of Perseverance** is a late fifteenth-century morality play. Forces representing good and evil were personified in characters on the stage: the Good Angels were the forces of goodness; and characters representing the forces of evil included the Bad Angels, the Devil and the Seven Deadly Sins. (The seven deadly sins are: pride, covetousness or greed, envy, wrath or anger, gluttony, sloth and lechery or lust.) You will see these characters incorporated into *Dr Faustus*.

B. **Everyman** is another morality play in which a man, representing the whole of mankind, is shown how to overcome temptation to achieve salvation. His great friend is Good Counsel, which means Good Advice, and in *Dr Faustus* this character becomes the Old Man.

What evidence of these morality features is there in *Dr Faustus*?

• At the very beginning of *Dr Faustus*, the Chorus speaks the prologue, which points out the theme of morality to the audience:

Only this, gentles: we must now perform
The form of Faustus' fortunes, good or bad.
And now to patient judgments we appeal,

The Chorus describes Faustus's merits, his rise and his fall.

- The forces of evil are represented on the stage by the Bad Angel, the devils, Lucifer, Mephostophilis, and Beelzebub.

- The forces of good are represented by the Good Angel and Old Man.

- When the Good and the Bad Angels appear on stage they are seen trying to persuade Faustus to behave in opposite ways. For example, the first time they appear in Scene 1 Faustus has become interested in necromancy. Marlowe calls the bad angel 'Spirit' to indicate a link with the devil and evil. They each address Faustus:

GOOD ANGEL   O Faustus, lay that damned book aside,
And gaze not on it lest it tempt thy soul
And heap God's heavy wrath upon thy head . . .

BAD ANG.   Go forward, Faustus, in that famous art
Wherein all nature's treasury is contained.

But there is something more complex going on here than simple persuasion. These angels actually represent Faustus's inner struggle. Whenever these angels appear, you should be aware that they are enacting Faustus's inner thoughts on stage.

ACTIVITY 1

Either go through the play and list the appearances of the Good and the Bad Angels, looking at who speaks first and why, and then work out what Faustus is thinking and feeling. **Or** use the above extract to work out what Faustus's inner thoughts are here:

GOOD ANGEL   Oh Faustus, if thou hadst given ear to me
Innumerable joys had followed thee.
But thou didst love the world.

BAD ANG.   Gave ear to me,
And now must taste hell's pains perpetually.

Look carefully at the verb 'hadst'; is it picked up by the Bad Angel?

- The parade of the Seven Deadly Sins in Scene 6 is used to show the audience Faustus's inner state of mind, and how he has deteriorated. He has no sense of the evil of the representations on stage, but finds them entertaining. Hence his response to each of them is lighthearted, for example, in his comments to Sloth:

FAUSTUS   And what are you, Mistress Minx, the seventh and last?

- The character of the Old Man is the equivalent of Good Counsel in *Everyman*. He tries hard to save Faustus from hell in Scene 18:

OLD MAN   Oh gentle Faustus, leave this damned art,
                This magic, that will charm thy soul to hell,

But it is too late because Faustus has given in to despair, ironically one of the Seven Deadly Sins he had laughed at earlier. Faustus now does not believe that God could forgive him, so he is destined for hell. The Old Man realises this:

OLD MAN   Accursed Faustus, miserable man,
                That from thy soul exclud'st the grace of heaven,
                And fliest the throne of his tribunal seat.

- The Chorus wraps up the play with an epilogue to sum it all up:

CHORUS   Cut is the branch that might have grown full straight,
                And burned is Apollo's laurel bough . . .
                Faustus is gone. Regard his hellish fall,

As you have seen, Marlowe has incorporated at least seven elements of the older morality play into *Dr Faustus*:

- the Chorus who spells out the moral of the play

- the forces of evil represented on stage

- the forces of good, the angel and the Old Man represented on stage

- the Good and the Bad Angels enacting Faustus's inner struggle

- the Seven Deadly Sins reveal Faustus's inner state of mind

- the Old Man as a giver of good advice

- The Chorus's epilogue summarises events.

Remember that this is only one Christian reading of the play related to this context; the final Chorus's speech is ambiguous, and could be a warning about falling into the same position as Faustus, who could not repent because of seeing things only one way. Likewise, you could regard the Old Man, or even the Good Angel, is less than useful to Faustus because they have taken only one view of his actions, and presume that the doctor is damned. In a non-Christian reading of the text, for example, the evidence would be assembled differently, and Faustus's death would be seen in other ways.

Faustus as Elizabethan tragic hero

Two types of contexts can be seen in this interpretation:

1 Elizabethan man as a tragic hero, within the social/historical context of the period in which the play was written

2 exploration of Faustus as a tragic hero in the context of dramatic genre.

There are certain charateristics of Faustus which you could examine here:

- He has achieved some status with his studies, but perhaps not as high a status as he would have liked.

- He is ambitious and proud of what he has done, but seems to be bored.

- He achieves through necromancy what he set out to do, but the consequences are not what he had imagined.

- He realises his plan has failed and is thrown into confusion, disappointment, and perhaps despair.

His status

Faustus's very first speech reveals a lot about his status and his achievements, ambitions and frustrations:

> FAUSTUS   Settle thy studies, Faustus, and begin
> To sound the depth of that thou wilt profess.
> Having commenced, be a divine in show,
> Yet level at the end of every art
> And live and die in Aristotle's works . . .
> Is 'to dispute well logic's chiefest end'?
> Affords this art no greater miracle?
> Then read no more: thou hast attained that end.
> A greater subject fits Faustus' wit.

ACTIVITY 2

You can see that already Dr Faustus had achieved much, but wants to go much further. How does Marlowe convey these ideas in this speech?

His ambitions

Even at the end of the first speech, Faustus is beginning to change his attitude towards magic and necromancy:

> Oh, what a world of profit and delight,
> Of power, of honour, of omnipotence,
> Is promised to the studious artizan!

Later, in Scene 3, Faustus has practised magic and believes that he has called up Mephostophilis:

FAUSTUS	Did not he charge thee to appear to me?
MEPHOSTOPHILIS	No, I came now hither of mine own accord.
FAUSTUS	Did not my conjuring speeches raise thee? Speak.

Although Mephostophilis explains that it was coincidence, Faustus will not listen to him, choosing to believe that his own new powers have worked.

ACTIVITY 3

1 Looking at both of these short speeches above, work out what you think Faustus's weaknesses are so far.

2 Try to pinpoint the ways in which his character has already begun to change.

Consequences of his decisions and actions

Even when Faustus is writing the pact and his blood congeals so that he cannot sign his name at first in Scene 5, he ignores the warning, and with this the chance to prevent his fall.

FAUSTUS	What might the staying of my blood portend? Is it unwilling I should write this bill?

ACTIVITY 4

Make a list of all the things that Faustus tells Mephostophilis that he wants.

The comic middle scenes of the play reveal to the audience just how little Faustus has achieved: Mephostophilis could not supply Faustus with any real knowledge, although they do time-travel together. Generally, you are made to see the pettiness of Faustus's new powers. He becomes a pathetic practical joker, conjuring little magic tricks for kings and dukes: tricking a horse-dealer and heckling the Pope. For example, Faustus is made invisible by Mephostophilis in Scene 9:

FAUSTUS	So, they are safe. Now Faustus, to the feast. The Pope had never such a frolic guest.
POPE	Lord Archbishop of Rheims, sit down with us.
BISHOP	I thank your Holiness.
FAUSTUS	Fall to, and the devil choke you an you spare.

This use of comic scenes is evident in much of Elizabethan and Jacobean drama and can be seen as a type of **generic context**. Such scenes have several purposes, including:

- amusing the audience

- developing the ideas in the main plot by enriching the themes, juxtaposing ideas, or turning the action of the main plot upside down.

ACTIVITY 5

Discuss what you think Marlowe is trying to achieve in these comic scenes. Why does Faustus seem to be damned?

ACTIVITY 6

1 What do you realise about Faustus's character now?

2 Look at his language again. Why do you think that he is made to speak in plain prose instead of the powerful poetry of earlier scenes?

3 What has he actually achieved and how have some of his grand plans and hopes been reversed?

The audience has become aware before Faustus, that he has achieved very little. This is called **dramatic irony**. As the realisation dawns, we see him in his final speech in Scene 19 in mental agony:

> FAUSTUS   Ah, Faustus,
> Now hast thou but one bare hour to live,
> And then thou must be damned perpetually . . .
> The stars move still, time runs, the clock will strike.
> The devil will come, and Faustus must be damned.
> Oh, I'll leap up to my God: who pulls me down?
> See, see, where Christ's blood streams in the firmament.
> One drop would save my soul, half a drop. Ah, my
> Christ! . . .
> No, Faustus, curse thyself, curse Lucifer,
> That hath deprived thee of the joys of heaven.

ACTIVITY 7

Faustus now recognises all that has happened. Write about the ways in which Marlowe portrays this recognition. You need to consider:

- the poetry of the language, the different registers and images

- the ways in which Faustus shows that he understands what has happened

- the ways in which you may think that he still does not understand.

Examine your response to Faustus. Do you feel any sympathy for him now? (Remember that the scene is discussed in terms of a Christian reading of the play.)

The Scholars then come on stage to describe Faustus's ghastly, grisly death. They are totally bewildered:

> FIRST SCHOLAR   Come, gentlemen, let us go visit Faustus,
> For such a dreadful night was never seen
> Since first the world's creation did begin.
> Such fearful shrieks and cries were never heard.
> Pray heaven the Doctor have escaped the danger.
>
> SECOND SCHOLAR   Oh, help us, heaven! See, here are Faustus' limbs,
> All torn asunder by the hand of death.

ACTIVITY 8

The Scholars say, 'Such fearful shrieks and cries were never heard':

1 Does this mean that Faustus's feared death did *not* happen? What are the implications of such an idea?

2 Why do the Scholars want to see Faustus? Who do you think that the Scholars are? What might their studies be?

3 Why does Marlowe use the Scholars to tell the audience about the death?

4 What do you think that the lesson of the play is?

5 Look carefully at the language of the Scholars: why do you think that Marlowe might make them plead to heaven and therefore to God?

6 Explore the two different language registers, that of religion and that of violence and violent acts. Why do you think that Marlowe has employed these two registers together?

7 Do you think that the actual tearing apart of Faustus may suggest that he is torn apart by split loyalties to God/ to evil, to love/ to fear?

8 Could Marlowe have had any other purposes here?

If you consider the words 'were never heard' you may open up another, non-Christian, reading of this play. Marlowe was known to have said that the only purpose of religion was to keep men in awe. An atheistic reading of the play could suggest that Faustus was not torn apart, and that what the play reveals is a cruel God, indifferent to the torment of Faustus, and indifferent to his repentance. Christian virtues would therefore be undermined. Such a reading would also form part of the moral context of the play (AO5i).

Restoration comedy – *The Country Wife* by William Wycherley

AO2i: knowledge and understanding of the text

In many ways, Wycherley's *The Country Wife* is a typical Restoration comedy. The basic plot is straightforward: Pinchwife, coming to London for his sister Alithea's wedding, brings his naïve young wife Margery with him. His suspicion and jealousy of her puts ideas into her head. In a parallel plot, Sparkish is due to marry Alithea, but his arrogance leads her to choose a new lover. Horner, a witty young, man persuades Pinchwife of his wife's innocence.

AO5i: the context to be explored here that is of morality

There are two basic critical positions in relation to Restoration drama. According to one, the writers have a concern for moral issues, but according to the other, the plays are largely crude and coarse comedy. This ambiguity may be seen, for example, in the character of Margery: her naïvety may be seen as a weakness in this society, and she could be seen as a victim.

AO3: how the writer expresses ideas related to this context

The names Pinchwife and Horner suggest links with morality drama in the way that they indicate the character's dramatic functions. For example, Pinchwife nearly has his wife pinched; Horner is engrossed with sex, and is in modern terms definitely horny!

Love is linked to money or to appetite. As Pinchwife says:

> He that shows his wife or money will be in
> danger of having them borrowed sometimes.

Horner is made to link the appetite for women to that for food:

> . . . for ceremony in love and eating is as
> ridiculous as in fighting; falling on briskly is all should
> be done in those occasions.

ACTIVITY 9

How does Wycherley link money and food to love or sex in the two short speeches above?

Horner and three of the female characters exchange explicit sexual banter in the famous 'china' scene:

[*Enter* LADY FIDGET *with a piece of china in her hand, and* HORNER *following.*]

LADY FIDGET	And I have been toiling and moiling for the prettiest piece of china, my dear.
HORNER	Nay, she has been too hard for me, do what I could.
MRS SQUEAMISH	O Lord, I'll have some china too. Good Mr Horner, don't think to give other people china and me none; come in with me too.
HORNER	Upon my honour, I have none left now.
MRS SQUEAMISH	Nay, nay, I have known you deny your china before now, but you shan't put me off so. Come –

HORNER	This lady had the last there.
LADY FIDGET	Yes, indeed, madam, to my certain knowledge he has no more left.
MRS SQUEAMISH	O, but it may be he may have some you could not find.
LADY FIDGET	What, d'ye think if he had had any left, I would not have had it too? For we women of quality never think we have china enough.
HORNER	Do not take it ill. I cannot make china for you all, but I will have a roll-wagon for you too, another time.
MRS SQUEAMISH	Thank you, dear toad.
LADY FIDGET	[to HORNER, aside] What do you mean by that promise?
HORNER	[apart to LADY FIDGET] Alas, she has an innocent, literal understanding.
OLD LADY SQUEAMISH	Poor Mr Horner, he has enough to do to please you all, I see.

*toiling and moiling means working extremely hard – a double entendre.
†roll-wagon is a goods-carrying vehicle. Here the word 'roll' also has a sexual connotation.

ACTIVITY 10

Work out and list as many of the double meanings in this speech as you can find, beginning with 'china'.

In a way, this extract sums up the tone of the play. On stage, in the *theatrical context*, it could be very funny. Horner and Lady Fidget appear on stage together. The stage directions read '*Enter* LADY FIDGET *with a piece of china in her hand*'. But from this point on in the exchange, 'china' has a sexual meaning, so the exchange rests upon **double entendre**. All the ladies talk about what Horner can offer them sexually.

ACTIVITY 11

Make a list of the ways in which each lady declares her interest in Horner and his sexual favours.

In the discussion in the extract, sex and appetite are clearly linked:

- china is a vessel for food; the play portrays sex as a social appetite
- china is fragile, smooth surfaced and man-made or artificial; society in this play is artificial, apparently polished but also fragile.

ACTIVITY 12

What does the extract tell you about the attitudes towards sexuality and morality displayed in this play?

There is a contrast to the general bawdiness of society in the lovers, Harcourt and Alithea. They have a different way of speaking when they talk of their love. Alithea believes that Sparkish loves her in an honourable and virtuous way:

Love proceeds from esteem; he cannot distrust my virtue. Besides, he loves me, or he would not marry me.

But Harcourt knows this is not true, and criticises Sparkish's materialistic attitude towards his fiancée, Alithea:

Marriage is rather a sign of interest than love; and he that marries a fortune covets a mistress, not loves her. But if you take marriage for a sign of love, take it from me immediately.

Later he talks of his love in religious terms, as if she were a saint, when he has begged her to postpone her marriage:

I could answer her, a reprieve for a day only often revokes a hasty doom; at worst, if she will not take mercy on me and let me marry her, I have at least the lover's second pleasure, hindering my rival's enjoyment, though but for a time.

ACTIVITY 13

Compare the different kinds of language used by the various characters in the short speeches above. What does this difference tell you about the attitudes of Alithea and Harcourt compared to those involved in the exchanges of the extract on page 97–8?

Alithea and Harcourt are two characters who are morally sound. Their love and respect for each other is apparent in the ways in which they act and speak. Their fidelity does not waver.

But the problem is that in *dramatic* terms, these characters are rather dull. They are not as lively or attractive as the 'vicious' characters engaged in the general pursuit of sex and money. These characters are not so realistic and are rather like the vice figures of the morality play. For example, it is doubtful whether Horner is meant to be seen as a fully rounded character. He is presented on stage in a one-dimensional way, as a personification of lust and extreme sexuality, rather like the parade of the Seven Deadly Sins in *Dr Faustus*. But nevertheless these characters have vitality.

Critics may say that either Wycherley was not very interested in conveying a moral, or there is a lack of balance between the two types of characters, 'vicious' and 'virtuous'. That is for you, the reader, to decide in the *moral context* of this play.

The comedy of manners – *The Rivals* by Richard Brinsley Sheridan

In *The Rivals*, first produced in 1773, Sheridan may on the surface appear to have picked up the good-natured comedy of some earlier Restoration comedy, but at the same time his writing is highly ambiguous.

> **AO2i: knowledge and understanding of the text**

In *The Rivals* there is the appearance of order, balance and symmetry which in some ways characterised the writing of the eighteenth century. As the name suggests, a comedy of manners is concerned with social behaviour. Here the plot is balanced, based on two courtships, Jack Absolute and Lydia Languish; Faulkland and Julia. Character types also seem to be balanced: two sensible characters, Absolute and Julia, and two romantics, Faulkland and Lydia. Because Lydia has a wilful fantasy about marrying a poor man, Absolute is forced to disguise himself as the penniless Ensign Beverley, which leads to the plot complications.

On the surface, there is a satire on the romantic sensibilities of Faulkland and Julia, but the play is much more serious than this. When you read *The Rivals* you should not be tricked into superficial judgements and consider the play simply as a comedy. There are some serious issues underlying the glittering surface. If you investigate these, you will realise that the play has tragic elements too.

> **AO5i: show understanding of the contexts in which literary texts are written and understood**

The two contexts to be considered here are drawn from the 'serious' areas of the play:

1 the *social context* of family, with consideration of parenting behaviour

2 the *moral context* of honesty and honourable behaviour.

(Remember that these are just two of the several contexts and readings you can find in this text.)

> **AO3: how the writer expresses ideas related to these contexts**

1 As examples of people with responsibilities towards the younger generation and their attitudes within this play, you could consider Sir Anthony Absolute and Mrs Malaprop. In the following extract, Sir Anthony has decided whom his son should marry and is trying to force Jack to agree:

> So you will fly out! Can't you be cool, like me? What the devil good can *passion* do? *Passion* is of no service, you impudent, insolent, overbearing reprobate! There you sneer again! Don't provoke me! But you rely upon the mildness of my temper. You do, you dog! You play upon the meekness of my disposition! Yet take care. The patience of a saint may be overcome at last! But mark! I give you six hours and a half to consider of this. If you then agree, without any condition, to do everything on earth that I choose, why, confound you, I may in time forgive you. If not, zounds, don't enter the same hemisphere with me! . . . I'll disown you, I'll disinherit you . . .

ACTIVITY 14

Look carefully at this speech and analyse Sir Anthony's attitude as a parent. You need to consider:

- the manner in which Sir Anthony speaks
- any contradictions between what Sir Anthony says and how he speaks
- how he regards his role as a father in caring for his son. Is it just? Is it wise? Is it caring?

Mrs Malaprop also has decidedly eccentric attitudes, evident, for example, when she talks of the education of a young woman:

> Observe me, Sir Anthony, I would by no means wish a daughter of mine to be a progeny of learning; I don't think so much learning becomes a young woman . . . I would send her, at nine years old, to a boarding-school, in order to learn a little ingenuity and artifice . . .

ACTIVITY 15

Look carefully at this speech and analyse Mrs Malaprop's attitude to young women. How wise is it? How just is it?

You can see an example of the misuse of language for which Mrs Malaprop is famous, in this extract, in her use of 'progeny'. But, in the case of the blustering Sir Anthony, you must look below the surface of the humour to spot the serious issues which Sheridan is concerned with. If you were to reassemble this evidence you could present a case for the *feminist context*, exploring what could be seen as the subservient role of women in the society of the age.

2 In the context of the critique of morality evident in this play, you need to examine the relationships between Absolute and Lydia, Faulkland and Julia. Lydia is wilfully romantic, wishing to reject a marriage which conforms to the normal expectations for a wealthy young woman of this period. When she finds out the penniless Beverley is in fact the wealthy Jack Absolute, she is horrified:

> So, while *I* fondly imagined we were deceiving my relations, and flattered myself that I should outwit and incense them *all*, behold, my hopes are to be crushed at once by my aunt's consent and approbation! And I am *myself* the only dupe at last! [*Taking a miniature from her bosom.*] But here, sir, is the picture – Beverley's picture! . . . [*flings it to him*] and be assured I throw the original from my heart as easily!

ACTIVITY 16

Look carefully at this speech and consider:

- What exactly are Lydia's motives in rejecting Jack?

- Are they the thoughts of a person who claims to love, and therefore to care for another?

Jack is so hurt and angry that he becomes involved in a duel, fortunately with no bad results. However, if the play had not had a comic purpose, the outcome of the duel could have been very different. The case is just as serious in the relationship between Julia and Faulkland. Faulkland, as wilful as Lydia, constantly winds himself up into a unwarranted state of jealousy over Julia. He taunts her with accusations that she does not love him until Julia, normally so forgiving and gentle, reaches breaking point:

JULIA   I know not whither your insinuations would tend. But as they seem pressing to insult me, I will spare you the regret of having done so. I have given you no cause for this! [*Exit* JULIA *in tears.*]

FAULKLAND   In tears! Stay, Julia. Stay but for a moment. The door is fastened! Julia! My soul! But for one moment. I hear her sobbing! 'Sdeath, what a brute am I to use her thus! Yet stay. Ay, she is coming now. How little resolution there is in woman! How a few soft words can turn them!

ACTIVITY 17

Look closely at this exchange. You need to consider:

* the effect of Faulkland's taunts on Julia

* Faulkland's words and manner of speech shown by the punctuation.

1 Is this the way to treat someone he claims to care for?

2 Does Faulkland realise his cruelty?

3 How does his tone change during this speech?

4 Does he seem to be consistent at all?

Faulkland's mood-swings are in evidence throughout the play. Julia has been badly hurt, which stands in sharp contrast to the comic mood of some moments in the play. The issue raised is about behaviour and responsibility towards another person. The conclusion to the play is just as ambiguous as the rest of the play. Julia's words end this 'comedy' as she talks of future happiness:

Then let us study to preserve it so; and while hope pictures to us a flattering scene of future bliss, let us deny its pencil those colours which are too bright to be lasting. When hearts deserving happiness would unite their fortunes, virtue would crown them with an unfading garland of modest, hurtless flowers; but ill-judging passion will force the gaudier rose into the wreath, whose thorn offends them when its leaves are dropped!

This ending is not really a comic ending; the tone is serious and rather sad. You have seen Faulkland throughout the play inflict great hurt; do you think he will change? Will the just Julia achieve the marriage she deserves?

ACTIVITY 18

Analyse Julia's final speech, and pick out the words which are rather solemn and may suggest doubt, such as the 'garland' which becomes a wreath. How optimistic do you find these closing words?

Of course, there are also the *comic contexts* within this play to be discussed, for example, the stock foolish characters and their posturing, such as Lucious O'Trigger and Bob Acres. But you need to be aware that Sheridan almost sets a trap for the unwary reader; lift up the layer of comedy, and you will find, amongst other things, a more serious consideration of how to treat, or indeed, how to hurt people who should be cared for, whether child or lover.

Summary

This section has looked at several different sorts of contexts in drama. You will have realised that those chosen for exploration in this module are examples, and that other contexts, and many other readings, are to be found within the plays. Use the models presented in this module to guide you through the play you are studying.

Post 1900 Drama

As explained in the introduction to this module, four Assessment Objectives are tested in this part of the examination paper. You will have to '*communicate clearly the knowledge, understanding and insight appropriate to literary study using appropriate terminology and accurate and coherent written expression*' (AO1), '*respond with knowledge and understanding*' (AO2i), '*show detailed understanding of the ways in which writers' choices of form, structure and language shape meanings*' (AO3), and '*articulate independent opinions and judgements informed by different interpretations of literary texts by other readers*' (AO4). The dominant Assessment Objective in this section is AO4, which carries 10 of the 20 marks available, with the other 10 marks split between the other three Objectives. A key consideration is AO3, however, as an understanding of the writers' skills and meanings will form the material for demonstrating AOs 2i and 3, and the basis for arriving at '*independent opinions and judgements*'. This section, therefore, will deal with these features first, before going on to consider how you can meet AO4 in the examination.

Form

One aspect of dramatic form is the way that actors can be used, in addition to their portrayal of characters. In Caryl Churchill's *Light Shining in Buckinghamshire*, for example, the actors sometimes speak in their own right, out of character:

1ST ACTOR	[*announces*] A Bill of Account of the most remarkable sufferings that the Diggers have met with since they began to dig the commons for the poor on George Hill in Surrey.
2ND ACTOR	We were fetched by above a hundred people who took away our spades, and some of them we never had again, and taken to prison at Walton.

The first speech is simply an announcement, though 'most remarkable' could be given some weight. Although the content and language of the second and subsequent speeches suggest characterisation as Diggers, there is no attempt to develop 'characters' from these short speeches.

One effect of this use of actors can be a more direct interaction with the audience, as they are not interacting with each other as characters. In the scene 'A Butcher Talks to his Customers' from *Light Shining in Buckinghamshire*, the Butcher is a clearly established character, in terms of feelings and attitudes, but is still not given a name or an audience onstage. He speaks only to the theatre audience.

Here is the end of the Butcher's speech:

It could be the food of life. If it goes into you, it's stink and death. So you can't have it. No, I said you can't have it, take your money back. You're not having meat again this week. You had your meat yesterday. Bacon on Monday. Beef on Sunday. Mutton chops on Saturday. There's no more meat for you. Porridge. Bread. Turnips. No meat for you this week. Not this year. You've had your lifetime's meat. All of you. All of you that can buy meat. You've had your meat. You've had their meat. You've had their meat that can't buy any meat. You've stolen their meat. Are you going to give it back? Are you going to put your hand in your pocket and give them back the price of their meat? I said give them back their meat. You cram yourselves with their children's meat. You cram yourselves with their dead children.

ACTIVITY 19

1 Pick out the words and phrases from the Butcher's speech above that suggest direct interaction with the audience.

2 Notice the rhetorical questions and commands. What effect might these have on the audience?

3 Pick out the emotive words and phrases, that are aimed at the audience's feelings.

4 One of Churchill's intentions in writing this play might have been to make the audience realise the social conditions at this time, and to think about rich and poor people. How has she used the Butcher to do this?

A narrator can be used by the writer to tell parts of the story, to fill in background, to indicate time changes, to comment on events and characters and to draw lessons for the audience, in other words, to 'frame' the action in a number of ways.

In *The Glass Menagerie*, Tennessee Williams uses the narrator, Tom, to do all of these things, and to act as a character in the drama himself. Here are some of his comments from his opening speech:

To begin with, I turn back time. I reverse it to that quaint period, the thirties, when the huge middle class of America was matriculating in a school for the blind.

As well as signalling the play's time-shift, Williams uses the narrator to give a socio-historical background, and the playwright's attitude to it. A further remark in the speech is: 'This is the social background of the play.'

The play is memory.
Being a memory play, it is dimly lighted, it is sentimental, it is not realistic.

Here, something of the nature and the mood of the play, and the dramatic presentation, are sketched in for the audience.

I am the narrator of the play, and also a character in it.

[*The gentleman caller*] . . . is the most realistic character in the play, being an emissary from a world of reality that we were somehow set apart from . . . since I have a poet's weakness for symbols, I am using this character also as a symbol.

There is a fifth character in the play who doesn't appear . . .

This is our father.

In this introductory speech the narrator is used to comment on the characters, including himself. There are also signals to the audience about the family's world of illusion, on the importance to the action of the character who doesn't appear, and on the symbolic significance of the gentleman caller; in this last function, the narrator is also speaking for the writer, perhaps.

Read the following extract from Scene 5 of *The Glass Menagerie* and then work through Activity 20.

TOM   [*to the audience*] Across the alley from us was the Paradise Dance Hall. On evenings in spring the windows and doors were open and the music came outdoors. Sometimes the lights were turned out except for a large glass sphere that hung from the ceiling. It would turn slowly about and filter the dusk with delicate rainbow colours. Then the orchestra played a waltz or a tango, something that had a slow and sensuous rhythm. Couples would come outside, to the relative privacy of the alley. You could see them kissing behind ash-pits and telegraph poles.
This was the compensation for lives that passed like mine, without any change or adventure.
Adventure and change were imminent in this year. They were waiting around the corner for all these kids.
Suspended in the mist over Berchtesgaden, caught in the folds of Chamberlain's umbrella –
In Spain there was Guernica!
But here there was only hot swing music and liquor, dance halls, bars, and movies, and sex that hung in the gloom like a chandelier and flooded the world with brief, deceptive rainbows . . .
All the world was waiting for bombardments!

ACTIVITY 20

Now try to analyse this passage and make notes on:

1 information given to the audience about place

2 creation of mood, as a background to the action

3 the narrator's own situation

4 information about the socio-historical context

5 how expectancy and tension are created in the audience.

Setting can also be suggested through stage directions, another aspect of dramatic form. The set itself is described in some detail in Tom Stoppard's play *Arcadia*, partly to suggest a time period, but it is also a set that is adapted for the two time periods in which the play is set. In *The Glass Menagerie*, the set is for the most part more naturalistic, with detail suggesting one period precisely. Part of the set, the fire escapes, also has a symbolic function that shapes meaning: 'all of these huge buildings are always burning with the slow and implacable fires of human desperation'. The opposite to this approach is seen in *Light Shining in Buckinghamshire*, where the only set is 'a table and six chairs', which enables a wider range of moods to be suggested to the audience more easily and quickly than by complete set changes. Props are also minimal in this play.

Tennessee Williams uses a screen on to which are projected images or legends, to shape meanings for the audience. Here is an example from Scene 1:

> AMANDA . . . Among my callers were some of the most prominent young planters of the Mississippi delta – planters and sons of planters!
>
> [TOM *motions for music and a spot of light on* AMANDA. *Her eyes lift, her face glows, her voice becomes rich and elegiac.*
>
> SCREEN LEGEND: 'OÙ SONT LES NEIGES'.]

The narrator is used here as a director of stage effects. The screen legend (a quotation from a nostalgic fifteenth-century French ballad by Villon) shows that Amanda's mind is deep in a memory of the past, but the mood of nostalgia evoked by the words of the poem, together with the stage directions to the actress playing Amanda, also invite a view of the character as lost in the past, feeling a deep sense of loss.

ACTIVITY 21

TOM: I like a lot of adventure.

[IMAGE ON SCREEN: SAILING VESSEL WITH JOLLY ROGER.]

AMANDA: Most young men find adventure in their careers.

Reading this short piece of dialogue, what does the sailing vessel suggest to you about Tom's desires? Why the *Jolly Roger*?

Contrast this with Tom's current existence, and think about the effect of Amanda's remark on the audience's view of the image, and of Tom.

Another device Williams uses is the transparent fourth wall, which ascends during the opening scene and descends again during the closing scene. Through this the audience observe the action, and the closed, isolated world in which Amanda and Laura live is emphasised. The possibility of release has been removed by the end of the play, as the wall descends once again.

Costume can be used to shape meanings about characters, as they are in both *Light Shining in Buckinghamshire* and *Arcadia*. Here is the description of Bernard's appearance from Act 1 Scene 2 of *Arcadia*:

Bernard, the visitor, wears a suit and a tie. His tendency is to dress flamboyantly, but he has damped it down for the occasion, slightly. A peacock-coloured display handkerchief boils over in his breast pocket . . .

Bernard's status as visitor, and as academic, is indicated by the suit and tie. The handkerchief 'boiling over' suggests his flamboyance and careless extravagance, which later leads him into trouble. Its peacock shades suggest a colourful nature, his brief disguise as Peacock (perhaps Chloë notices the colour, or its message, when she invents this name for him) is echoed later in his knowledge of Thomas Peacock. Stoppard also uses costume to confuse the two time periods, by having the modern characters dress up in fancy dress, i.e. costumes belonging to the earlier period, for the ball. At this point, the action from the two periods is occurring on stage simultaneously as well, leading the audience to consider parallels, differences, and the passage of time.

Music is also used in drama to create various effects to help shape meanings. The bible verses, sung by the whole company, that open *Light Shining in Buckinghamshire*, for example, might create an apocalyptic mood, but they also create a sense of the harmony of the company. In *Arcadia*, music is used very subtly by Stoppard to underscore and comment on the action, and to provide illustrations of ideas. In Act 1 Scene 4, as Valentine and Hannah begin to discuss mathematical models, the audience hear from the next room 'a piano . . . beginning to play quietly, unobtrusively, improvisationally'. Several pages on,

Valentine, trying to describe the difficulty of finding the equation, says: 'Like a piano in the next room, it's playing your song, but unfortunately it's out of whack, some of the strings are missing, and the pianist is tone deaf and drunk'. He then describes how you pick the tune out of the noise by experimenting until you find it. The sound of the piano offstage provides a background to his words which informs the audience's understanding of the idea, perhaps even subconsciously. Valentine describes Thomasina's work as 'playing with numbers . . . doodling'.

> HANNAH   A monkey at a typewriter?
>
> VALENTINE Yes. Well, a piano.

Here is the exchange when the piano is heard again:

> HANNAH   What is he playing?
>
> VALENTINE I don't know. He makes it up.
>
> HANNAH   Chloë called him 'genius'.

This time the playing is commented on directly, and thus not only develops further the audience's view of the mysteriously silent Gus, who communicates through the piano, but also draws attention to the parallel between Gus and Septimus – 'the genius of the place' – and to Thomasina.

Music is used extensively by Tennessee Williams in *The Glass Menagerie*, largely, as he says in the Production Notes, 'to give emotional emphasis to suitable passages'. In Scene 5, for example, the stage direction '*The Dance-Hall music changes to a tango that has a minor and somewhat ominous tone*' clearly indicates the way music is being used. As a dramatist, Williams also makes careful use of sound effects.

This passage from Scene 6 of *The Glass Menagerie* shows a number of stage effects working together. The shy, withdrawn Laura is being called in to meet a 'gentleman caller' whom she knows, and doesn't want to face.

> AMANDA: You're keeping us waiting, honey! We can't say grace until you come to the table!
>
> [*The back door is pushed weakly open and* LAURA *comes in. She is obviously quite faint, her lips trembling, her eyes wide and staring. She moves unsteadily toward the table.*
> LEGEND : 'TERROR!'
> *Outside a summer storm is coming abruptly. The white curtains billow inward at the windows and there is a sorrowful murmur and deep blue dusk.*

> LAURA *suddenly stumbles – she catches at a chair with a faint moan.*]
>
> TOM: Laura!
>
> AMANDA: Laura!
>
> [*There is a clap of thunder.*
>
> LEGEND: 'AH!']

ACTIVITY 22

Examine the ways in which the various elements in this passage – the legends, the storm, the movement of the curtains, the sound effect of the murmur, the colours, and the thunder – create the atmosphere which underscores the emotions of the characters on stage.

Arcadia uses sound effects, including music at the end of the play, to suggest time, the movement between periods of times, and the parallels between the two time frames. At the end of Act 1, which finishes with a modern scene, there is this stage direction before the curtain:

> *The light changes to early morning. From a long way off, there is a pistol shot. A moment later there is the cry of dozens of crows disturbed from the unseen trees.*

Knowing of the potential duel in the nineteenth-century scene, suspense is created in the audience, which is first thwarted by the Interval, and then by Act 2 beginning with a twentieth-century scene. When Scene 6 opens, it is with:

> *A reprise: early morning – a distant pistol shot – the sound of the crows.*

The feeling of suspense returns, briefly, to be dissipated when Septimus enters with pistols. He has shot a brace of rabbits, apparently. The sound effect here creates a bridge between the two time frames but is ultimately used for humorous effect.

A prop is used to create dramatic irony in *Arcadia*, when Hannah looks at the sketch book, which also links the two time periods. She comments on the likeness of the Sidley hermit, saying that it was 'drawn in by a later hand, of course'. The audience alone know that it was drawn in by Thomasina at the time, because they saw it. The irony adds to the shaping of meaning in terms of the interpretation of evidence. Similarly, in *Light Shining in Buckinghamshire* the vicar's hypocrisy is shown through the wine:

VICAR	'Be afflicted and mourn and weep.' That is the way to heaven.
SERVANT	Sir.
	[*He pours more wine.*]

Stage directions are usually employed to indicate movements, but can also be used subtly to add to meaning.

In this next passage from Scene 7 of *Arcadia*, characters from both time periods are on the stage at the same time – Lady Croom and Septimus from the nineteenth century, and Chloë and Valentine from the twentieth. Thomasina (nineteenth) and Hannah (twentieth) remain seated at the table throughout.

	. . . LADY CROOM *enters from the music room, seeming surprised and slightly flustered to find the schoolroom occupied. She collects herself, closing the door behind her. And remains watching, aimless and discreet, as though not wanting to interrupt the lesson.* SEPTIMUS *has stood, and she nods him back into his chair.*
	CHLOË, *in Regency dress, enters from the door opposite the music room. She takes in* VALENTINE *and* HANNAH *but crosses without pausing to the music room door.*]
CHLOË	Oh! – where's Gus?
VALENTINE	Dunno.
	[CHLOË *goes into the music room.*]
LADY CROOM	[*Annoyed*] Oh! – Mr Noakes's engine!
	[*She goes to the garden door and steps outside.*
	CHLOE *re-enters.*]
CHLOË	Damn.
LADY CROOM	[*Calls out*] Mr Noakes!
VALENTINE	He was there not long ago . . .
LADY CROOM	Halloo!
CHLOË	Well, he has to be in the photograph – is he dressed?
HANNAH	Is Bernard back?
CHLOË	No – he's late!
	[*The piano is heard again, under the noise of the steam engine.* LADY CROOM *steps back into the room.*
	CHLOË *steps outside the garden door. Shouts*] Gus!

LADY CROOM	I wonder you can teach against such a disturbance and I am sorry for it, Mr Hodge.
	[CHLOË *comes back inside.*]
VALENTINE	[*Getting up*] Stop ordering everybody about.
LADY CROOM	It is an unendurable noise.
VALENTINE:	The photographer will wait.
	[*But, grumbling, he follows* CHLOË *out of the door she came in by, and closes the door behind them.* HANNAH *remains absorbed . . .*]

ACTIVITY 23

1 If you are working in a group, try playing the scene according to the stage directions, with the music room door and the other door on opposite sides of the stage, the table centre, and the garden doors upstage. You'll see how the action has to intersect, just as the time frames are doing, and how the characters' movements echo each other.

2 Chloë is in Regency dress. What difference does this make?

3 Look at all the dialogue, and work out how comments and replies in one time frame seem to refer to dialogue in the other.

4 What effect is achieved by having Hannah and Thomasina remain at the table?

Structure

'Structure' refers to the variety of techniques the dramatist has used in constructing the play, which help to shape meanings for the audience. The use of the 'fourth wall' in *The Glass Menagerie*, which was mentioned on page 109, has a structural significance. Because the audience has seen the wall being removed at the beginning, when it descends in the last scene a sense of closure is produced. This is doubly significant as Amanda and Laura have both been offered a possibility of escape during the action, only to be closed in again by the end.

Finding structures in a play (or a poem or a novel) is best achieved by thinking about patterns, for example, where similar scenes or combinations of characters or dialogue recur, and perhaps change. In *Light Shining in Buckinghamshire* there are two scenes between Briggs, a working man, and Star, who is recruiting for the army. The first scene, 'Briggs joins up', begins with Star remarking that Briggs keeps his hat on, and ends:

STAR	Very good, Briggs. Excellent. Now one thing. You wear your hat. Will you take orders?
BRIGGS	If they're not against God.
STAR	They can't be against God in God's army.

The use of the hat at the end of the scene is a structural device, as the scene begins and ends with it, and Star interprets it as a symbol of Briggs's willingness to bow to authority. The two meet again towards the end of the play, by which time much has changed.

Here are two excerpts from the end of the second scene:

BRIGGS	God is not with this army.
STAR	It is the army of saints.
BRIGGS	And God's saints shot Robert Lockyer for mutiny. By martial law. In time of peace. For demanding what God demanded we fight for.

and

BRIGGS	It's you who mutiny. Against God. Against the people.
STAR	Briggs.
BRIGGS	It's Cromwell mutinies.
STAR	Briggs.
BRIGGS	If I was Irish I'd be your enemy. And I am.
STAR	Briggs.
BRIGGS	Sir.

ACTIVITY 24

Compare the extract from the first scene with the two extracts from the second scene.

1   How has the relationship between Briggs and Star changed?

2   How has Briggs's perception of God's relationship with the army changed?

3   What is Star's attitude to Briggs here, do you think?

In drama, decisions have to be taken by the director and actors about how to play particular lines and moments. Given what you've seen so far, would Briggs be wearing his hat here? How do you think Briggs should say 'Sir' – submissively? Defiantly? The choice makes a big difference to the interpretation of this scene, and perhaps the play as a whole.

In the same play a similar structural technique produces a different effect. The vicar appears in two scenes. In the first, mentioned on page 112, he is speaking to his servant, and talks of the necessity of evicting tenants if they don't submit and come to church. In the second, towards the end of the play, as he is talking to Star, the new landlord, it becomes clear that the vicar is still willing to have tenants evicted if they don't submit to the new landlord's rents. This time the scene is a mirror image of the first; despite the war, nothing has changed at all, which is one of the meanings that the writer is leading the audience towards. When the vicar says 'I welcome all the changes you are making' and 'I'm not against change', these remarks become ironic in the light of the earlier scene.

In *Arcadia*, Tom Stoppard mirrors dialogue between the two time periods to help the audience see the parallels. In Act 2 Scene 2, for example, Lady Croom remarks to Septimus 'I do not know when I have received a more unusual compliment'. In Act 2 Scene 3, only five minutes or so later in playing time, Hannah says to Valentine 'I don't know when I've received a more unusual proposal'. Similarly, Thomasina's 'Am I the first person to have thought of this?' in the first scene is echoed almost exactly by Chloë in Act 2 Scene 3. In both cases, a production might well choose to echo the positions on stage of the speakers to underline the parallel. Stoppard uses objects to link scenes, as well; for instance, Gus presents Hannah with an apple at the end of Act 1 Scene 2, and at the beginning of Scene 3 an apple is on the table, 'the same apple from all appearances'. Septimus then cuts it up and eats it.

Time is an element in most plays, and writers use a variety of structures to deal with it. *Light Shining in Buckinghamshire* deals with some of the events of the Civil War, and proceeds chronologically through them. Because 'each scene can be seen as a separate event rather than part of a story' (Caryl Churchill's introduction), however, the passage of time is indicated by devices such as accounts of particular events by actors, or changes in character's attitudes, as shown in Activity 24.

The structure of *Arcadia* is built around the switches from the nineteenth to the twentieth century and back, with both time frames appearing on the stage together in the final scene. The way this works in detail is suggested by the sketch book of Mr Noakes. In this '*the pages, drawn in watercolours, show "before" and "after" views of the landscape, and the pages are cunningly cut to allow the latter to be superimposed over portions of the former*'. In the same way, scenes and moments are repeated in the two time frames.

In *The Glass Menagerie* Tennessee Williams uses Tom, the narrator, to explore the theme of time. In his opening speech he says: 'To begin with, I turn back time. I reverse it to that quaint period, the thirties, when the huge middle class of time was matriculating in a school for the blind'. Tom signals his structural role here and also, in the second sentence, there is an indication of how it will happen, when he switches from present tense, 'I reverse' to past tense, 'was matriculating'.

ACTIVITY 25

The Glass Menagerie is a 'memory play'. At the end, the play emerges from memories:

TOM   . . . It always came upon me unawares, taking me altogether by surprise. Perhaps it was a familiar bit of music. Perhaps it was only a piece of transparent glass –
Perhaps I am walking along a street at night . . .

1 Why might the music or the glass evoke memories, and take Tom into the past again?

2 How is the switch back from past time to present time shown?

The narrator links the scenes in *The Glass Menagerie*, and even when he doesn't, the scenes flow from one to the next in an uninterrupted chronological sequence. The opposite of this is seen in *Light Shining in Buckinghamshire*, where little connection is made between one scene and the next, and 'characters are not played by the same actors each time they appear'. This is a structural device which shapes meaning: as Caryl Churchill says, 'this seems to reflect better the reality of large events like war and revolution where many people share the same kind of experience'.

Scenes may be structured internally, as suggested by the treatment of Briggs's hat on page 114. Another example from *Light Shining in Buckinghamshire* is in 'A Butcher talks to his customers', quoted on page 106 which begins with the Butcher politely offering his customers meat, and ends with 'You cram yourselves with their dead children'. The scene is structured like this to shape the writer's meaning. Dialogue can be structured for effect too, as in the interlocking speeches from the different time frames in *Arcadia*, shown on pages 112–113.

Language

One of the functions of language in drama is to convey character. Here are the first words of Brotherton in 'Brotherton meets the Man', the fifth scene of *Light Shining in Buckinghamshire*:

> Went up the road about a mile then I come back. There's a dog not tied up. So I started back where I slept last night. But that was into the wind. So I'm stopping here. It's not my shoes. I've got better shoes for walking in my bag. My sister's shoes that's dead. They wouldn't fit you. How much you got?

Brotherton's simplicity is conveyed by short sentences and simple, repetitive diction and syntax. Her first sentence starts without 'I', and the question at the end is simple and direct. Her conversation is about life's necessities – shelter, walking, shoes, sleeping, money. She knows little else, as we see from the rest of the play.

This is a speech by Claxton about water, from 'Claxton brings Hoskins home' from the same play.

> Fish can live in it. Men can't. Now men can't live here either. How we live is like the sea. We can't breathe. Our squire, he's like a fish. Looks like a fish too, if you saw him. And parson. Parson can breath. He swims about, waggles his tail. Bitter water and he lives in it. Bailiff. Justices, Hangman. Lawyer. Mayor. All the gentry. Swimming about. We can't live in it. We drown. I'm a drowned man.

His last words in the scene are:

> We can't live. We are dead. Bitter water. There shall be a new heaven. And a new earth. And no more sea.

There are several language features here, which help to establish Claxton's character and his state of mind, and have a bearing on the meanings of the play.

ACTIVITY 26

1 Look at the sentences in Claxton's speech. What do you notice about the length and syntax?

2 Are Claxton's words simple or sophisticated? What have these two features told you about Claxton?

3 What does Claxton compare the lives of the other characters to? How does he use these comparisons to reflect on their hardships?

4 Look carefully at the movement of thought between one sentence and the next. Do they all follow each other logically? What does this tell you about Claxton?

As in poetry or prose, **figurative language** is used by writers to make the audience reflect on meanings. Tennessee Williams, for example, uses symbolism extensively in *The Glass Menagerie*. In his opening speech the narrator says he has 'a poet's weakness for symbols', and that the gentleman caller should be seen as a symbol. The importance of the glass menagerie as a symbol for Laura and her life is signalled by its use in the title, and Laura mentions that she has been spending most of her time in 'that big glass-house' – a phrase the audience might well be reminded of when the transparent fourth wall descends at the end of the play. She is described as she is preparing for Jim's visit as being '*like a piece of translucent glass touched by light, given a momentary radiance, not actual, not lasting*'. The hope that Jim brings will not last, either. When the glass unicorn's horn is broken, Laura says 'Now it is just like all the other horses', and that it will feel 'less – freakish!' Clearly the glass animal is a symbol of Laura herself here.

In Scene 4 of *The Glass Menagerie*, Tom describes the magician's stage act.

TOM . . . But the wonderfullest trick of all was the coffin trick. We nailed him into a coffin and he got out of the coffin without removing one nail. [*He has come inside.*] There is a trick that would come in handy for me – get out of this 2 by 4 situation! . . . You know it don't take much intelligence to get yourself into a nailed-up coffin, Laura. But who in hell ever got himself out of one without removing one nail?

[*As if in answer, the father's grinning photograph lights up.*]

ACTIVITY 27

1 When does Tom first liken his situation to being in a coffin?

2 How are the family 'nailed-up' by their situation?

3 How did the father get out of the 'coffin'?

4 If the coffin symbolises the family's situation, and their apartment, how might the audience interpret the descent of the wall at the end of the play? Remember throughout all this the obvious connotations of the word 'coffin'.

One characteristic of Stoppard's language in *Arcadia* is word play. Here is the exchange when Chater challenges Septimus to a duel for making love to his wife, for example.

CHATER	You dare to call me that. I demand satisfaction!
SEPTIMUS	Mrs Chater demanded satisfaction and now you are demanding satisfaction. I cannot spend my time day and night satisfying the demands of the Chater family. As for your wife's reputation, it stands where it ever stood.
CHATER	You blackguard!

Septimus plays on Chater's phrase 'demand satisfaction' to refer to a completely different sort of satisfaction, and makes his remark about Mrs Chater's reputation sound like a compliment. Chater, however, recognises that he means the exact opposite.

Here are the opening words of the play:

THOMASINA	Septimus, what is carnal embrace?
SEPTIMUS	Carnal embrace is the practice of throwing one's arms around a side of beef.
THOMASINA	Is that all?
SEPTIMUS	No . . . A shoulder of mutton, a haunch of venison well hugged, an embrace of grouse . . . *caro*, *carnis*; feminine; flesh.

ACTIVITY 28

- In this extract Septimus tries to avoid the answer to Thomasina's question by playing on the words 'carnal' and 'embrace'. How does he play on both of these in his definition?

- Look carefully at how he continues these ideas in the second speech. Although this word play produces humour, that isn't its sole function. Think about the relationship it starts to establish between Thomasina and Septimus. What sort of relationship is it? What mood is being set up for the play in these opening lines?

Plays might also contain different language **registers,** depending on their subjects. *Light Shining in Buckinghamshire*, for example, is full of the biblical language of prayers and sermons, which reflects one of the central issues of the play. In *Arcadia*, there are registers belonging to mathematics, physics, landscape gardening, literary study and art, amongst others, reflecting the diversity of subjects that Stoppard yokes together in the play.

> **AO4: articulate independent opinions and judgements informed by different interpretations of literary texts by other readers**

This is the most important Assessment Objective for the twentieth-century texts on this paper, carrying 10 of the 20 marks available. Questions are likely to give a view of the text and the writer, and ask for your opinion. A question might well direct you to one particular scene to think about. Before considering how you might plan your answer, it's worth thinking about the kinds of subjects that might crop up. Broadly, they could focus on the writer's concerns, and how the writer presents them; the writer's techniques; or the qualities of the writer's work. Here is a list of some of the things which could form the focus of questions about Caryl Churchill, Tom Stoppard and Tennessee Williams. This is not an exhaustive list, by any means.

Light Shining in Buckinghamshire

- the position of women in society

- divisions between rich and poor

- how the writer uses the historical context

- the nature of liberty

- the nature of religion

- the failure of revolution

- Churchill's uses of form, language and structure.

Arcadia

- how Stoppard uses the second law of thermodynamics

- how Stoppard uses chaos theory

- literary study/the nature of evidence

- how Stoppard creates and uses time frames

- how Stoppard creates humour.

The Glass Menagerie

- illusions

- the American Dream

- the grip of the past

- Williams's use of stage directions and effect

- Williams's use of symbolism.

Forming a response

As an example, let's suppose that you were studying *Arcadia*, and that the question you were going to tackle was:

'*A critic considered that the ending to* Arcadia *demonstrates Stoppard's craft, but also his coldness in finishing the play with a thought about the demonstration of the second law of thermodynamics. Do you agree with this view? Consider the last page of the play, from Bernard's exit.*'

You know that:

- you have to consider the critic's view

- you have to write about form, structure and language, not just meanings – the word 'craft' tells you this

- you must come to an 'independent opinion' about the effect of the ending.

There are a number of ways to structure your response, but you would need to think about some of these issues:

- the effect of the lighting of the candlestick – the audience know about Thomasina's death on that night

- the contents of the table – when Thomasina puts the candle on the table, and Hannah sits at it, the debris of the action of the play in both time periods is visible

- the switch to piano music is a further reminder of the way the action of the play has moved between the two time frames

- Gus appears in Regency dress, so it is not clear which Gus this is until he speaks; a further reminder of both characters, and the movement between time periods

- Septimus's line 'Be careful with the flame' is a further reminder of Thomasina's fate, and the alpha 'in blind faith' of her genius

- the dancing reminds the audience of Thomasina's response to the prospect of extinction – 'then we will dance!' – a lead up to the law of thermodynamics

- the drawing of 'Septimus holding Plautus' is what Hannah's 'blind faith' required – it is the proof of the identity of the Sidley Hermit – Septimus, who is dancing on the stage. It is Gus, the inheritor of Thomasina's genius, who gives it to her

- the dancing of the two couples creates a harmony between the two periods, which ends when the play finishes.

There is obviously plenty of material here and throughout the play about Stoppard's craft, through which you could demonstrate your knowledge of his dramatic techniques.

The critic's view about the 'coldness' of the ending was presumably based on the knowledge of Thomasina's death by fire after the end of the play. You could agree with this, of course, and show your understanding of the way this idea is used in the play. You need to consider *different interpretations of literary texts*, though, so you might offer the view that the crafting of this last scene, with the dancing of the couples to piano music, the romance between Septimus and Thomasina, and the audience's knowledge of her death, is unlikely to lead the audience into a consideration of the second law of thermodynamics at this moment.

Pre 1900 Poetry

The same Assessment Objectives (AO1, AO2i, AO3, AO5i) are tested in the Pre 1900 Poetry as in the Pre 1900 Drama with Assessment Objective 5i dominant.

Exploring Pre 1900 Poetry

In this section on Pre 1900 Poetry you will consider a number of different contexts:

- the context of period and genre

- historical context

- various social contexts, including religious and moral contexts, and love relationships

- a biographical context.

You will be using skills to study the poetry in this module similar to those you used to look at Pre 1900 Drama. You should ask yourself some of the same questions that you asked about drama:

- what different *contexts* can I find within the poetry?

- how has the writer used *form, structure and language* to convey the ideas and experience within these contexts?

The Canterbury Tales by Geoffrey Chaucer – The Wife of Bath's Prologue and Tale

The Canterbury Tales comprises a series of stories told by pilgrims on their journey from London to Canterbury. As these tales were written towards the end of the fourteenth century they fall into the category of medieval literature. In this section we will look at some of the ideas and traditions which provided the context for Chaucer's writings and the influences on his use of language and verse forms.

(As in the Drama section there are several other contexts within the poetry apart from those used as examples in this book. There are also different readings of the text other than those discussed in this book.)

Context: period and genre

Some of the ideas behind Chaucer's poetry are derived from a form known as the Romance, which reflected the concerns of medieval society. There were two clear codes of conduct for the ideal knight: **Courtly love**, which specified rules of behaviour towards a woman whom a knight wished to 'court', and the **Chivalric code**, which laid down rules for the ways in which a knight should behave on and off the battlefield.

According to the traditions of courtly love, a knight must worship his lady, who should remain remote, mysterious, aloof and chaste. Sexual conquest was not supposed to happen until a large number of rituals had been gone through. These ideas were drawn from French literature, notably *The Romance of the Rose* which explored the spiritual aspects of love.

According to the chivalric code, the knight at the same time owed duties of loyalty and brotherly love to his leader and his fellow knights. Loyalty to them was sacred. The result was that a knight was subject to two sets of rules, one of love and one of war, which often caused conflicts of loyalty and behaviour.

This conflict, and other sorts of conflict, lie at the heart of *The Canterbury Tales* as Chaucer explores the contradictions and difficulties of various aspects of medieval society.

Within the *period context* of the courtly code of behaviour, Chaucer presents the conflict between the actual experience of everyday life and the ideal as presented in literature. For example, what the Wife of Bath experiences is a far cry from the ideal love-relationship of the Romances. The husbands themselves are often parodies of the knight as courtly lover.

All the relationships with the Wife of Bath's husbands are seen to be aggressive, and in this way parody 'ideal' behaviour, as with her fifth husband Janekyn:

> Now wol I seye yow sooth, by Seint Thomas,
> Why that I rente out of his book a leef,
> For which he smoot me so that I was deef.

ACTIVITY 29

1 What sort of marital relationship is presented here by the Wife of Bath?

2 Is Janekyn behaving like a courtly knight and lover?

3 Why do you think that Chaucer makes the Wife tear out the page?

ACTIVITY 30

Now look through your text and try to pick out the different conflicts that occur.

1 Are any of these related to either of the two codes of conduct, the courtly or the chivalric?

2 What might Chaucer be saying about courtly love in relation to harsh reality?

3 Does he think the codes of conduct should be ignored – or that they are out of date?

Chaucer also refers to the church teachings of the time, and moral rules drawn from literature and sets these against the actual experience of his characters. The conflict between the ideal codes of behaviour drawn from biblical teaching and actual practice appears throughout *The Canterbury Tales*. In *The Wife of Bath's Prologue and Tale* Chaucer presents the conflicts between the 'experience' of the Wife, and what may be seen as the heartless teachings of the Church, led by dry old men. He also explores the conflict between a woman's point of view generally and the point of view of the anti-female clerics or church officers.

At the beginning of *The Wife of Bath's Prologue* Chaucer uses the Wife to make this opposition clear:

Experience, though noon auctoritee
Were in this world, is right ynogh for me
To speke of wo that is in mariage;

ACTIVITY 31

1 What point of view is the Wife expressing here?

2 Why do you think that Chaucer makes the word 'experience' the very first word of the *Prologue* to her *Tale*?

The Wife of Bath systematically contradicts the Church's teaching of the time by undermining or disputing religious texts:

I nyl envye no virginitee.
Lat hem be breed of pured whete-seed,
And lat us wyves hoten barly-breed;
And yet with barly-breed, Mark telle kan,
Oure Lord Jhesu refresshed many a man.

She uses historical evidence to back up her point of view:

Lo, heer, the wise kyng, daun Salomon:
I trowe he hadde wyves mo than oon.

ACTIVITY 32

How exactly does the Wife use the biblical text and historical example to support her case?

This opposition between actual experience and the ideals of courtly love and the teachings of the Bible and Church elders can also be seen in the relationship of *The Wife of Bath's Prologue* to her *Tale*.

ACTIVITY 33

Compare the situations and outcomes within the *Wife of Bath's Prologue*

But atte laste, with muchel care and wo,
We fille acorded by us selven two.

with that at the end of her *Tale*:

'Thanne have I gete of yow maistre,' quod she,
'Sin I may chese and governe as me leste?'
'Ye, certes, wyf,' quod he, 'I holde it beste.'
'Kis me', quod she, 'we be no longer wrothe;
For, by my trouth I wol be to you bothe fair and goode.

1 What sort of relationships are established between wives and husbands at the end of the *Prologue* and the *Tale*?

2 Look at the words which Chaucer uses, such as 'care and wo' and 'kis', 'fair and good'. Why does he use different registers?

3 Are the outcomes the same, or do they differ in some ways?

4 Is Chaucer suggesting that the *Tale* is some sort of wish-fulfilment of the Wife's?

Structure

The medieval influence on *The Canterbury Tales* is not just restricted to the ideas but also extends to the structure. There is a different sort of method of construction at work here. In modern times we tend to expect a logical and clearly sequenced piece of literature. But the medieval mind did not work like this. Think of an old cathedral like Durham or Wells or Winchester – perhaps you could look at a picture of one. The building is a mass of different styles: outside there will be those curving, supporting arches, known as flying buttresses, next to intricate carved statues; inside there may be a real mishmash of styles. There will be intricate little statues in niches again, and large statues, delicate filigree designs on the plaster of the walls, and huge soaring plain arches. All the component parts will be different, but the overall effect is of a beautiful and majestic building.

ACTIVITY 34

Look at the photographs of the inside and outside of Salisbury Cathedral, and note the different styles that you see.

Chaucer constructed his poetry from a combination of different styles, use of flashbacks and changes of tense, contradictions, a mixture of language from the homely and colloquial to formal literary language, ambiguity and irony, and of course, a key word in Chaucer, the use of **digressions**. All these elements are **interlaced** to give the final tapestry effect of the poem's form and structure.

Chaucer's use of language

Irony is important in a discussion of Chaucer's work; it is a sophisticated form of sarcasm, in which the real meaning of a phrase is disguised behind another. Chaucer frequently mocks his own characters in *The Canterbury Tales* by use of irony.

In *The Wife of Bath's Prologue and Tale* Chaucer's use of irony is abundant, as is his use of ambiguity, as the Wife frequently contradicts herself or says things which are ironically ambiguous, such as:

> Al were he short, or long, or blak, or whit:
> I took no kep, so that he liked me

ACTIVITY 35

1 Work out the two possible meanings of the phrase 'so that he liked me'.

2 What opposite qualities do they suggest about the character of the Wife?

Chaucer's style makes use of exaggeration, puns and scholarly language. The Wife of Bath refers regularly to the Gospels, learned texts and history. This may seem out of character for a humble wife, but Chaucer makes us believe that the learned Janekyn imparted this knowledge to her.

Such a wide range of reference opens up a new perspective on the words of the Wife. They also bring other contexts into focus within the poetry. Such references can be used as evidence in your discussions of *social, religious, moral contexts and historical contexts*, including:

- the attitudes and teachings of the Church

- the education of the time

- the position of women within the society

- the concept of 'maistre'.

Chaucer's use of **digression** in a similar way. They occur when Chaucer or the storyteller seems to ramble off the point, but in fact, like the embroidery around a medieval tapestry, they serve to illustrate the ideas of the *Tale*. The Wife of Bath frequently interrupts her argument to digress, for example at line 323 when she seems to drift off to talk about Ptolemy, and line 951 when she talks about Midas with his ass's ears:

> He loved hire moost, and trusted hire also;
> He preyede hire that to no creature
> She sholde tellen of his disfigure.

The Wife 'kan no conseil hide', and lets the secret out.

ACTIVITY 36

1 How does this digression relate to the ideas in the *Prologue* and *Tale*?

2 What does it suggest about the character of the Wife?

3 What does it imply about the nature of women?

4 Why do you think that Chaucer makes the Wife appear to condemn herself out of her own mouth?

5 What does it tell you about the position of women within the social context of the period?

In Chaucer's poetry there are often two processes occurring at the same time: there is the progress of the tale itself, and there are sideways movements to elaborate upon various points, as in the use of 'digressions'. This is part of Chaucer's 'interlacing' effect.

As in any poetry, the **imagery** that Chaucer uses supports the meaning of the poem. In *The Wife of Bath's Prologue and Tale* there is much animal imagery, usually applied to the Wife herself. She is as jolly as a magpie or bites like a horse, for example. This seems to suit the Wife as she sees herself having more to do with flesh and animality than with the spirit.

ACTIVITY 37

Make a list of the animal images which you can find in *The Wife of Bath's Prologue and Tale*. Work out why Chaucer uses these images and the effect they have upon you. Here is one to begin with:

> Thou seydest this, that I was lyk a cat;
> For whoso wolde senge a cattes skyn,
> Thanne wolde the cat wel dwellen in his in;
> And if the cattes skyn be slyk and gay,
> But forth she wole, er any day be dawed,
> To shewe hir skyn, and goon a-caterwawed.

1 How does the Wife use this example to argue her point?

2 What does it reveal about her attitudes?

3 What does it suggest about women generally within the social context of the period?

The *form* of the *General Prologue* and a considerable part of the *Tales* is that of the **heroic couplet**, that is, iambic pentameters rhymed in pairs. Iambic pentameter is a line with five weakly stressed syllables each followed by a strong one; the lines are rhymed in pairs. Here is an example:

And eek I praye Jhesu shorte hir lyves
That noght wol be governed by hir wyves;
And olde and angry nygardes of dispence,
God sende hem soone verray pestilence!

ACTIVITY 38

Work out the effects of the use of the heroic couplet in the extract above.

1 What is the effect of the rhyme by bringing certain words together?

2 How does the metre help to convey meaning?

3 What do you learn of the character of the Wife of Bath here?

4 Do you think that Chaucer is using any irony when he puts this language into her mouth at the end of a 'serious' tale?

All the characteristics of Chaucer's poetry discussed above form part of the *context of genre*. Other contexts include the historical and social contexts of the relationship between real life and a literary ideal; the woman's role within these two worlds; and the period contexts of ideas and of structure.

The poetry of Elizabeth Barrett Browning

Elizabeth Barrett Browning wrote many types of poetry, but she has become most famous for her sequence of sonnets, *Sonnets From the Portuguese*. Robert Browning called Elizabeth his 'Portuguese girl' in his love poems to her, a kind of secret code. So she returns the favour with this sequence. Here is one of her sonnets, 'If Thou Must Love Me':

If thou must love me, let it be for nought
Except for love's sake only. Do not say
'I love her for her smile . . . her look . . . her way
Of speaking gently, . . . for a trick of thought
That falls in well with mine, and certes brought
A sense of pleasant ease on such a day' –
For these things in themselves, Belovèd, may
Be changed, or change for thee, – and love, so wrought,
May be unwrought so. Neither love me for
Thine own dear pity's wiping my cheeks dry, –
A creature might forget to weep, who bore
Thy comfort long, and lose thy love thereby!
But love me for love's sake, that evermore
Thou mayst love on, through love's eternity.

The contexts to be considered here are the *social context of love*, and also the *biographical context*, since the poet wrote this as a token of her own love (AO5i).

AO2i: knowledge and understanding of the poem

The poet writes here about the state of being in love. She thinks about what it is to be in love, how time may change things, and what the nature of true love really is.

AO3: how the writer expresses the ideas related to these contexts

---

You will see that the poem consists of a series of linked ideas.

ACTIVITY 39

Look at the ways in which the poet presents her ideas on what it is to love and to be loved. You need to think about:

- the sequence of ideas

- the ways in which the poet refers to aspects of herself, such as her smile, her looks, her voice

- what worries her about her lover's feelings

- the ways in which the last two lines draw the sonnet to a conclusion

- the use of direct address and the effects this creates

- the use of full rhyme, such as 'say/way'

- the use of half rhyme, such as 'thereby/eternity'

- the register

- the tone of the poem.

This poem explores what it means and what it feels like to be in love, which forms part of the *social context of love*.

Read through another of these sonnets from the same sequence and work through Activity 40.

Say over again, and yet once over again,
That thou dost love me. Though the word repeated
Should seem 'a cuckoo-song', as thou dost treat it,
Remember, never to the hill and plain,
Valley and wood, without her cuckoo-strain,
Comes the fresh Spring in all her green completed.
Beloved, I, amid the darkness greeted,
By a doubtful spirit-voice, in that doubt's pain
Cry . . . 'Speak once more . . . thou lovest!' Who can fear
Too many stars, though each in heaven shall roll –
Too many flowers, though each shall crown the year?
Say thou dost love me, love me, love me – toll
The silver iterance! – only minding, dear,
To love me also in silence, with thy soul.

ACTIVITY 40

Analyse the ideas about love and loving expressed in this poem, and the ways in which the writer expresses these ideas. You should:

- trace the sequence of the poet's thoughts

- look at the ways in which the poet defines love

- consider the use of dialogue

- consider the use of repetition in the language – how does it develop the ideas of the poem? (The word 'iterance' means repetition.)

- consider the tone of the poem.

But Elizabeth Barrett Browning had concerns other than love. Like the other Victorian writers in the prescribed selection she was very much concerned with social and moral issues, which provided another set of contexts for her poetry.

In her poem 'The Runaway Slave at Pilgrim's Point', she presents the hardship suffered by black slaves, exemplified by a young black woman who is forced to kill her child. Contexts with the poem include the social, the *moral* and from a modern perspective, the *historical* context related to slavery.

In this poem a young black woman is raped and gives birth to a half-caste child whom she kills. The death of the child is treated apparently casually; after twisting him in her shawl to kill him, she looks inside the bundle:

> Too suddenly still and mute.
> I felt, beside, a stiffening cold:
> I dared to lift up just a fold, . . .
>   As in lifting a leaf of the mango-fruit.

ACTIVITY 41

1 Who is speaking here in the extract above?

2 What are the advantages of having the slave woman speak?

3 Who does the 'stiffening cold' refer to? Is it the dying child or the mother?

4 Look at the language in these lines, especially the image of the mango leaf. What does this suggest about the cultural context?

5 Why does the poet compare lifting the shawl to see the dead child to lifting a mango leaf?

The image of the fruit is developed in the next stanza, where there is a sharp change of tone.

> But *my* fruit . . . ha, ha! – there, had been
>   (I laugh to think on't at this hour!)
> Your fine white angels (who have seen
>   Nearest the secret of God's power)
> And plucked my fruit to make them wine,
> And sucked the soul of that child of mine,
>   As the humming-bird sucks the soul of the flower.

Within the social, religious, moral and historical contexts Elizabeth Barrett Browning heightens the reader's awareness of the suffering endured by the slave woman.

ACTIVITY 42

How does the poet dramatise the woman's responses in the verse above? You need to consider:

- the punning on 'fruit'

- the tone of voice – is the laugh bitter?

1 Does she feel excluded from the world of the white men who have angels, 'your angels'?

2 Does she perhaps feel excluded from the care of the angels?

3 Does the reference to humming-birds indicate a cultural context?

4 Does she feel that the life of a black child 'gathered to make them wine' has no value?

In her poem 'The Cry of the Children', Elizabeth Barrett Browning explores further social injustices; here the contexts are again *moral*, *social* and framed within the *historical context* of the Industrial Revolution.

'For, all day, the wheels are droning, turning, –
    Their wind comes in our faces, –
Till our hearts turn, – our head, with pulses burning,
    And the walls turn in their places:
Turns the sky in the high window blank and reeling,
    Turns the long light that drops adown the wall,
Turn the black flies that crawl along the ceiling,
    All are turning, all day, and we with all.

In this extract, the 'we' refers to the young children employed in the mills. As in the previous poem, the poet uses dramatic language, but this time with two speaking voices. There is the speaker critical of the situation, addressing the 'brothers' who allow it to occur, and of course the general reader. There is also the voice of the young children speaking for themselves and for future 'lost' generations.

ACTIVITY 43

How is the *industrial context* conveyed in the extract above? How effectively is this done? You need to consider:

- the repetition of the word 'turn'. What effect does this create?

- the quality of nightmare conveyed by the sense of movement and by words such as 'the black flies'

- references to matters of health, such as 'pulses burning' and 'reeling'

- the idea of nature reversed, as in the 'wind' being the draught from the machinery.

There is some degree of *biographical context* here too, as when she wrote this poem Elizabeth Barrett Browning was herself fevered and dying from consumption.

In 'Christmas Gifts' there is again a *historical context* in the focus on an Italian uprising against an unjust papacy. The range of contexts is similar – *social*, *moral* and also *religious.*

The poem is a **parody** of the three kings' gifts to Christ, the *generic context*. The corrupt Pope is handed an Italian socialist flag as a gift:

– O mystic tricolor bright!
    The Pope's heart quailed like a man's:
The cardinals froze at the sight,
    Bowing their tonsures hoary:
And the eyes in the peacock-fans
    Winked at the alien glory.

*tonsures are the monks' trimmed heads.
†peacock-fans are used in papal processions.

ACTIVITY 44

How does the poet convey the historical and moral contexts in this extract?

1 Why is the flag described as 'mystic'?

2 Why do the Pope and his cardinals 'quail' at the sight of the people's flag? Why do they have processions with peacock-fans?

3 Why does the poet personify the peacocks so that they have to close their eyes at the sight of the flag?

4 Where do you think that the poet's sympathies lie?

As you have seen, there are many different contexts evident in Elizabeth Barrett Browning's poetry, and a few of these have been considered as examples. The ideas related to these contexts are conveyed in a great variety of ways, including the **dramatic monologue**, which is something the poet shares in common with her husband Robert Browning.

The poetry of Robert Browning

Robert Browning uses dramatic poetry to great effect in creating his monologues. He makes his characters speak for themselves, and as they do so, they reveal their faults in humorous ways.

In his poem 'The Bishop Orders his Tomb at Saint Praxed's Church', we are given a clear picture of a bishop who is most unholy. In fact he is lecherous, greedy, money-minded and jealous. Although the effect is humorous, there is a serious message here as Browning condemns by ridicule the church of his day. The following three extracts show how Browning makes the man condemn himself out of his own mouth:

> Vanity, saith the preacher, vanity!
> Draw round my bed: is Anselm keeping back?
> Nephews – sons mine . . . ah God, I know not! Well –
> She, men would have to be your mother once,
> Old Gandolf envied me, so fair she was!

AO2i: knowledge and understanding of the poem

Browning uses ridicule and satire to achieve his effect here. A dying bishop admits to fathering children by a beautiful woman. Gandolf is jealous. Is he another corrupt bishop? Did he carry on in the same way? Obviously this man wants to make his death a dramatic affair, to be the centre of attention.

The contexts to be considered in this poem are:

- the *generic contexts* of satire and of the dramatic monologue

- the *social contexts* of religion and morality with the serious criticisms which Browning makes in these areas.

AO3: how the writer expresses the ideas related to these contexts

---

A particular register is used to establish the speaking voice of the bishop; the dashes and exclamation marks suggest the rhythms of the spoken voice. Exclamation marks indicate how excitable he is in this situation which he sees as urgent. The language is **colloquial** – the language of everyday speech. It is not the formal language of a deathbed statement from a dying bishop. His attitude and behaviour is inappropriate for the situation, just as we assume that this behaviour has been during his life.

A few lines later the bishop gives orders about where he wants his tomb to be:

> And so, about this tomb of mine. I fought
> With tooth and nail to save my niche, ye know:
> – Old Gandolf cozened me, despite my care;
> Shrewd was that snatch from out the corner South
> He graced his carrion with, God curse the same!

Browning reveals a little more of the bishop's character here; not only did he have love affairs, he is also vain and jealous. He wanted his tomb to be in the best place, but Gandolf, who obviously wanted the same, beat him to it. The language is not that of a holy man. He shouldn't have 'fought' over such vain things; he is certainly not holy in finishing with a curse!

He has also, we discover later, hoarded possessions away secretly: houses and a precious piece of blue stone called lapis lazuli. To make his tomb look more impressive:

> Sons, all have I bequeathed you, villas, all,
> That brave Frascati villa with its bath,
> So, let the blue lump poise between my knees,
> Like God the Father's globe on both his hands
> Ye worship in the Jesu Church so gay, . . .

ACTIVITY 45

1 Re-read the last extract and consider what you have learned about the bishop here.

2 Look at the language, for example, the comparison the bishop makes to God. What does Browning reveal about the bishop's character?

3 How does the bishop condemn himself in these lines?

Now look at all the extracts together and think about the *contexts of religion and morality*. What criticisms can you find in the poem about the church of the day and the behaviour of its ministers? You need to think about issues such as:

- vanity
- greed
- unbrotherly spite, malice and envy.
- materialism
- unlawful sex

You may well conclude that, despite the humour, there is a very serious criticism being made in this poem. On the other hand, you may feel that Browning's humour makes the bishop seem likeable in a way, that within the contexts of religion and morality the criticism is lightened by the humorous approach.

There are also many different contexts to be found in Browning's poem 'Bishop Blougram's Apology'. ('Apology' means here a justification of personal beliefs and attitudes.) Although there may be many other contexts and readings to be explored, the principal ones are:

- the debate between faith and doubt, a typically Victorian characteristic which is part of the *context of period*

- the criticism of the Church and its ministers which you have seen in the previous poem, the *moral and religious contexts* (the poem is said to be a portrait of Cardinal Wiseman, the Archbishop of Canterbury)

- a sideswipe at the hack-journalists of the day, which is a *social context*.

The following two extracts exemplify the first two types of context. Here Blougram is speaking:

> The sum of all is – yes, my doubt is great,
> My faith's the greater, . . .

ACTIVITY 46

How do these words form part of the context of the debate of the period between faith and doubt?

Here the bishop offers a clear and frank statement about his philosophy.

> Of course you are remarking all this time
> How narrowly and grossly I view life,
> Respect the creature-comforts, care to rule
> The masses, and regard complacently
> 'The cabin,' in our phrase! Well, I do.
> I act for, talk for, live for this world now,
> As this world prizes action, life and talk:
> No prejudice to what next world may prove, . . .

ACTIVITY 47

What are the implications of the bishop's words? You need to think about:

- how the bishop thinks of this life as a preparation for the next

- how spiritual or material his view is

- why Browning has him speak with such disarming honesty

- whether this self-knowledge and honesty undermines your criticism of the bishop as humour did in the previous poem.

In discussing the bishop's views you are addressing the *religious context* of the faith and doubt of the period; in addressing Browning's technique you are engaging with the *context of genre* – how this particular type of satirical poem is written.

In considering Browning's mockery of hack-journalism you are considering one aspect of the *social context*. Here is an extract from the poem where Blougram speaks to the interviewing journalist, Gigadibs:

You, Gigadibs, who, thirty years of age,
Write stately for Blackwood's Magazine,
Believe you see two points in Hamlet's soul
Unseized by the Germans yet – which view you'll print –
Meantime the best you have to show being still
That lively lightsome article we took
Almost for the true Dickens . . .
And pleased a month, and brought you in ten pounds.

ACTIVITY 48

What does Browning imply here about journalism and scholarship? You need to think about:

- the value of the work Gigadibs does

- the jealousies between academics of England and Germany

- the use of the word 'lightsome': what does it suggest about the writing?

- the use of the word 'almost'

- Gigadibs's motives in writing the pieces.

Elsewhere in his poetry Browning continues the Victorian debate between faith and doubt, the *context of period*. In his poem 'Apparent Failure' he deals with three bodies fished out of the River Seine. This prompts the speaker to think about his own faith.

My own hope is, a sun will pierce
The thickest cloud earth ever stretched;
   That, after Last, returns the First,
Though a wide compass round be fetched;
   That what began best, can't end worst,
Nor what God blessed once, prove accurst.

ACTIVITY 49

Facing the bodies of the dead, the speaker ponders what happens after death. He wonders whether the cloud will lift to achieve the sun of salvation and be blessed by God.

What consolation and faith does the speaker manage to achieve? You need to consider:

- what the 'cloud' could be

- what God blessed in the first place

- what is the 'Last' event?

- what can the 'First' be?

- how the speaker finds consolation. Does he reason this out, or is it a simple act of faith?

- what effects Browning has created by using a speaker to address the reader.

In these poems, you have seen that Browning engages in typically Victorian considerations of faith, doubt and morality. These are central issues related to the *context of the period*. In examining how Browning has created effects in his poetry, you have considered the *context of genre*. You have seen that one of the essential characteristics of Browning's poetry is the dramatic quality of his verse. This is also one of the central characteristics of Tennyson's narrative poetry.

The poetry of Alfred Lord Tennyson

Narrative poetry

Many writers of poetry tell a story in their poems, often about themselves. In narrative poetry the writers set out specifically to tell a tale or to narrate a story to the reader.

Tennyson wrote many narrative poems, including some extended poems such as *Maud*. Tennyson called this poem a monodrama because there is just one speaker. One of the questions to ask about narrative poetry is 'How does it hold the reader's interest?' There are two answers: first, by the content of the story itself, and secondly by variation in the style in which the story is told. These considerations are part of the *context of genre.*

AO2i: knowledge and understanding of the poem

Maud tells the story of the life and loves of the narrator, who goes through a series of extreme changes of mind and mood during the course of the poem. At first he is depressed because of a series of dire family events; then he falls in love with Maud and becomes happy; then he loses her and falls into a kind of madness again. Finally he finds some consolation in the love of his country.

All these changes are signalled by variations in the ways in which Tennyson uses language and structure, so that language and sound effects ring the changes throughout the poem. In this extract from the beginning of the poem, the narrator is distraught about the evil things that have happened to his family:

> I hate the dreadful hollow behind the little wood,
> Its lips in the field above are dabbled with blood-red heath,
> The red-ribb'd ledges drip with a silent horror of blood,
> And Echo there, whatever is ask'd her, answers 'Death'.

This is a very dramatic opening to the poem. We realise that the man is deeply disturbed, and that a murder (that of his father, we find out later) has been committed.

AO5i: the contexts to be considered are the generic context of narrative verse, and social, in the ideas of love and of violent death

---

ACTIVITY 50

How does Tennyson present the horror of the violent killing in this extract? You need to think about:

- how Tennyson presents nature in this extract

- his use of personification, for example, in his use of the words 'lips'

- the register, for example, in his use of words such as 'hate', 'dreadful', 'blood', 'death'

- the dramatic tone of the speaker's voice

- how he appeals to all the senses.

How has Tennyson made you feel about the murder?

In this next stanza you will see that the mood has changed completely. The concern with murder and death has been replaced by a concern with love. Here you can consider a different *social context*, that of love.

But now shine on, and what care I,
Who in this stormy gulf have found a pearl
The countercharm of space and hollow sky,
And do accept my madness, and would die
To save from some slight shame one simple girl.

ACTIVITY 51

Analyse the effects which Tennyson creates in this extract. You need to consider:

- the attitude and ideas of the narrator and his change of mood

- what he appears to feel about the power of love

- the use of imagery, such as the pearl

- the use of language, including the effects created by alliteration and sibilance

- the effectiveness of the rhythm and rhyme scheme.

The social contexts of the poem expand as Tennyson goes on to consider the duty of defending one's country, a motif which is also typical of several Victorian writers. Read this next extract from *Maud* and work through Activity 52 below.

Friend, to be struck by the public foe,
Then to strike him and lay him low,
That were a public merit, far,
Whatever the Quaker holds, from sin;
But the red life spilt for a private blow –
I swear to you, lawful and lawless war
Are scarcely even akin.

ACTIVITY 52

What does Tennyson have to say about the morality of war in this extract? You need to think about:

- the justification of fighting in war – who strikes first?

- the morality of this action

- the attitude towards those who object to this course of action

- differences between private and public morality

- the tone of the speaker

- the wordplay and effects created by the opposition of 'lawful' and 'lawless'.

Elsewhere in his poetry Tennyson explores the universal human situation in which man tests his abilities to the limit. In these poems there are several contexts available for exploration: the *historical and literary context* in the use of myth, and the *moral context* in which mankind is presented as strenuously trying to improve his life.

In his poem 'Ulysses' Tennyson explores the attitudes of the Greek hero to his journeys, using Ulysses as the speaker.

I am a part of all that I have met;
Yet all experience is an arch wherethro'
Gleams that untravell'd world, whose margin fades
For ever and for ever when I move.

ACTIVITY 53

What is Tennyson saying about human life here? You need to consider:

- the value of experience

- whether man can attain absolute knowledge and experience

- whether in the end man is fated to continue to struggle, without ever reaching his goal.

This theme of man's continual struggle is repeated throughout the poem, as Tennyson explores the human condition. Look at this second extract:

> And this grey spirit yearning in desire
> To follow knowledge, like a sinking star,
> Beyond the utmost bound of human thought.

There is an ambiguity in these lines that could reinforce the idea that man must struggle, but even so may not finally achieve what he would like to.

ACTIVITY 54

Look at the language in these lines above and consider how Tennyson expresses his ideas about the condition of mankind – and the moral and social contexts in which he sets his poem.

1 Consider the impact of the phrase 'sinking star'. Is it wise to follow such a star?

2 Could it lead to death, perhaps, as the star sinks?

3 Is it even possible to go beyond the 'bound of human thought'?

Later in this poem, Ulysses is made to speak heroic words:

> One equal temper of heroic hearts,
> Made weak by time and fate, but strong in will
> To strive, to seek, to find, and not to yield.

Tennyson seems to make his view on the human condition clear here. He also provokes the reader into an emotional and sympathetic response.

ACTIVITY 55

What do you think about what Tennyson says in the lines above and the way he expresses it? You need to consider:

- the use of the word 'heroic'

- deliberate oppositions established in the language, such as weak/strong and strive/seek/not to yield

- what Tennyson, using Ulysses as an example, suggests is the value of the struggle, the outcome or even the effort itself

- whether this effort should cease as age approaches.

Tennyson addressed the universal problem of growing old and facing death, a frequent motif in his poetry. This can be seen as another of the *social and moral contexts* in his poetry. This next extract from the 'Choric Song' of 'The Lotos-Eaters' echoes the theme of 'Ulysses', as a group of sailors grow tired of travelling and battling through life, and have lost the will to struggle on:

> Is there any peace
> In ever climbing up the climbing wave?
> All things have rest, and ripen toward the grave
> In silence; ripen, fall and cease:
> Give us long rest or death, dark death, or dreamful ease.

ACTIVITY 56

What is Tennyson suggesting here? You need to think about:

- whether old age offers any relief from the struggles of life

- whether Tennyson accepts the stern Victorian philosophy of work and duty – a central motif of much Victorian poetry.

Finally, it is worth looking at the *context of genre* in Tennyson's poetry.

ACTIVITY 57

Using the same extract, consider how Tennyson has crafted his poetry, using the following devices to support his theme:

- variations in the pattern of rhythm and rhyme, and of line length

- use of vowels and consonants to establish the tone

- use of contrasts – 'ripen/death' for example

- use of repetition to create effects.

You have explored some of the contexts in Tennyson's poetry, such as private issues of love and death, and public themes of war, duty and struggle. This combination of contexts may also be found in the poetry of Christina Rossetti.

The poetry of Christina Rossetti

Christina Rossetti's poetry is wide-ranging in its interests and techniques. The first context to be considered is the context of love. This is a *social context*, but also a *biographical context* as Rossetti herself suffered the pangs of unrequited love.

Her poem 'A Birthday' is a song celebrating love:

My heart is like a singing bird
　　Whose nest is in a watered shoot;
My heart is like an apple tree
　　Whose boughs are bent with thickset fruit;
My heart is like a rainbow shell
　　That paddles in a halcyon sea;
My heart is gladder than all these
　　Because my love is come to me.

Raise me a dais of silk and down;
　　Hang it with vair and purple dyes;
Carve it in doves and pomegranates,
　　And peacocks with a hundred eyes;
Work it in gold and silver grapes,
　　In leaves and silver fleurs-de-lys;
Because the birthday of my life
　　Is come, my love is come to me.

*vair is a decorated fur.
†fleurs-de-lys are emblems used in heraldry.

ACTIVITY 58

What does Christina Rossetti have to say about the feeling of being in love in the first stanza? You need to think about:

- the series of pictorial images, such as the bird and the tree and the shell

- the use of repetition

- the build-up to the comparison in the last line of this stanza

- the appeal to all of the senses

- the varied rhyme schemes

- the use of a regular rhythm.

In the second stanza, the poet changes tone and pace. Instead of looking at 'my' love, she describes more objectively the state of being in love.

ACTIVITY 59

How does Christina Rossetti develop her ideas about love in the second stanza of this poem? You need to think about:

- the use of images of queenliness

- the use of texture and of colour

- the use of the senses

- the various meanings of the word 'birthday'.

Christina Rossetti's poetry is diverse in its subject-matter and themes. At times she is keen observer of nature, with a sharp eye for detail, as illustrated in this next extract from her poem 'Spring'.

There is no time like Spring
When life's alive in everything,
Before new nestlings sing,
Before cleft swallows speed their journey back
Along the trackless track –
God guides their wing, . . .

ACTIVITY 60

What observations does Christina Rossetti make about nature here. You could consider:

- the use of the birds as images of spring

- the simplicity of the language

- the sense of celebration of life.

There is obviously another important theme in this extract, that of religion. Rossetti builds up to the idea of God controlling the spring.

ACTIVITY 61

1 What impression do you get of God's guidance in this poem?

2 Do you think that the poem could be more than just a celebration of spring?

Christina Rossetti wrote much religious poetry, and was also concerned with the idea of death. Here are the first and last verses from a poem called 'Up-hill'. This provides a contrast to the previous poem and may seem to be more like a hymn than a song:

Does the road wind up-hill all the way?
   Yes, to the very end.
Will the day's journey take the whole long day?
   From morn to night, my friend . . .

Shall I find comfort, travel-sore and weak?
   Of labour you shall find the sum.
Will there be beds for me and all who seek?
   Yea, beds for all who come.

AO2i: knowledge and understanding of the poem

The poem is **allegorical**, it is about mankind's journey through life to death and salvation, or 'comfort'. The word allegorical suggests that although the poet is talking about a journey, there is another deeper level of meaning implied.

AO5i: the context to be considered is the religious context

AO3: how the writer expresses the ideas related to this context

- The writer uses **dialogue** to convey her ideas. One voice asks questions, and the second voice answers them. This gives a dramatic feeling to the poem.

- The rhythm varies with each speaker.

- The voice of the first speaker, who asks the questions, is given a four-stressed line, longer than that of the second speaker. This helps to suggest the difficulty of the 'up-hill' journey through life.

- The lines given to the second speaker are shorter, with three stresses, perhaps to suggest the ease felt on arrival.

- The language of the first speaker emphasises the effort: 'up-hill', 'all', 'whole', 'long'.

- The language is slightly **archaic**, or deliberately old-fashioned, and solemn: 'morn' and 'my friend'.

- This register recalls the language of hymns, as it talks of achieving rest in heaven and establishes the *religious context* of the poem.

ACTIVITY 62

Using the model above, analyse the second stanza in this extract.

The contexts you have looked at in the poetry of Christina Rossetti include those of love, nature and religion. There are also other contexts you could consider, as well as other readings of the poems.

Post 1900 Poetry

As explained in the introduction to this Poetry section, four Assessment Objectives are tested in this part of the examination paper. You will have to 'communicate clearly the knowledge and understanding appropriate to literary study using appropriate terminology and accurate and coherent written expression' (AO1), 'respond with knowledge and understanding' (AO2i), 'show detailed understanding of the ways in which writers' choices of form, structure and language shape meanings' (AO3), and 'articulate independent opinions and judgements informed by different interpretations of literary texts by other readers' (AO4). The dominant Assessment Objective in this section is AO4, which carries 10 of the 20 marks available, with the other 10 marks split between the other three objectives. A key consideration is AO3, however, as an understanding of the writers' skills and meanings will form the material for demonstrating AOs 2i and 3, and the basis for arriving at 'independent opinions and judgements'. This section, therefore, will deal with these features first, before going on to consider how you can meet AO4 in the examination.

Form

An obvious feature of form in any poem is rhyme, or variations of it, or no rhyme at all, all of which are deliberate choices. As rhyme connects things, full rhyme might be used to establish a sense of certainty, of things belonging. Here are two lines from U. A. Fanthorpe's 'Under the Motorway':

> Petrol and diesel will both dry up
> But that doesn't happen to a Buttercup.

In the poem the writer suggests that what 'lies in wait' when the motor car has had its day is 'seeds'. The certainty of this is shaped by the sureness of 'doesn't happen', by arranging the sentence so that an end-stopped line after 'Buttercup' ends it, and by the full rhyme, underlined by the stop.

ACTIVITY 63

Read the last two lines from the poem:

> Rolls Royce and Volvo, their day is done,
> But Charlock and Dandelion blaze in the sun.

1 How is certainty suggested here? Think about the capital letters, the effect of the word 'blaze', and the rhyme.

2 Why are these two words ('done' and 'sun') linked at the end of the poem, which is about flowers lasting?

Half-rhyme can be used for a variety of purposes, such as creating a sense of dissatisfaction, of things not being right, as in this verse from Philip Larkin's 'Toads Revisited':

All dodging the toad work
By being stupid or weak.
Think of being them!
Hearing the hours chime, . . .

As the speaker considers what it would be like not to work, the unsatisfactory prospect is conveyed by the half-rhyme in 'work/weak'; it is really little more than an echo, as in 'them/chime'.

ACTIVITY 64

Here are the last two lines of 'Toads Revisited':

Give me your arm, old toad;
Help me down Cemetery Road.

The poem is dominated by half-rhymes, but ends on a full rhyme, 'toad'/'Road'. Why do you think the poet does this? Think about what has been suggested about certainty.

You should also look for **internal rhymes**. Carol Ann Duffy's 'Welltread', for instance, begins:

Welltread was Head and the Head's face was a fist.

'Tread' and 'Head' form a full rhyme, underlined by the repetition of 'Head'. His hardness and misplaced certainty is established in the first three words.

Rhythm is important too, when it is used to shape meaning. Look at the last line in 'Under the Motorway', quoted in Activity 63 above. The sense of everything being in its place, or rather re-established as such, is complemented by the steadiness of the rhythm there.

ACTIVITY 65

Here is the last line of 'Welltread':

There was the burn of a cane in my palm, still smouldering.

The narrator is describing being caned. Listen carefully to the rhythm of the line. Where do the stresses fall? How many times is the hand hit, do you think? How do you know?

The ends and beginnings of lines and stanzas can also be used to create effects. In 'The Whitsun Weddings', for instance, the break created by 'Hedges dipped/And rose' in the second stanza matches the visual up-and-down effect which Larkin is describing. In Duffy's 'Disgrace', the third stanza ends with 'nothing we would not do to make it worse', and the fourth begins 'and worse'. The space between the stanzas emphasises the never-ending arguments between the couple.

ACTIVITY 66

Look at the space between the first and second stanzas of Larkin's 'Dockery and Son':

I try the door of where I used to live:
Locked. The lawn spreads dazzlingly wide.

What effect is created by the gap here? Notice the effect of the colon before the break, too. How is 'Locked' made to seem so final?

The length of lines can be manipulated to control pace. In Larkin's 'Here', for example, the first three stanzas, comprising 24 lines, describe a railway journey, and the lines form one continuous sentence, flowing through line and stanza divisions. Here is the end of the third stanza and the beginning of the fourth:

Isolate villages, where removed lives

Loneliness clarifies. Here silence stands
Like heat. Here leaves unnoticed thicken,

At the 25th line, 'Loneliness clarifies', the verse suddenly halts at a full stop. Three words later the word 'stands' suggests a lack of movement at the end of the line, followed by a pause on the line break, two monosyllabic words, and another full stop, followed by a repetition of the word 'Here' – the poem has arrived at a static place.

ACTIVITY 67

Look at these lines from 'The Whitsun Weddings':

We ran
Behind the backs of houses, crossed a street
Of blinding windscreens . . .

And at this line:

A slow and stopping curve southwards we kept.

1   Look where the line divisions come in the first extract. How do these keep the lines flowing?

2   Which words suggest movement?

3   In the single line, there is still movement, but it's slow. Which words suggest slow movement, or lack of movement?

4   What effect does the repetition of the letter 's' (this is called **alliteration**) have?

5   What effect does the full stop at the end of the line have? (This is what is meant by 'an **end-stopped** line'.)

Another feature of form is the creation of voices within poems. In 'The Room Where Everyone Goes' for instance, Fanthorpe italicises '*Ooh, look! The loo/the toilet/the bog*' to suggest the voices of sundry visitors, while '*Despatched by the hand of God*', presented in the same way, suggests both the diction and the evasiveness of the 'careful cleric'.

Carol Ann Duffy makes frequent use of italics to suggest a different voice. At the end of 'Litany' she presents her own voice, as a child, in:

A boy in the playground, I said, *told me*
to fuck off; . . .

The insertion of 'I said' here creates a slight delay before she reveals to the reader the word she repeats to her mother's friends, thus anticipating the 'thrilled, malicious pause'.

ACTIVITY 68

At the beginning of 'Litany' Duffy uses italics to present the women's small-talk:

candlewick
bedspread three piece suite display cabinet –

1   What punctuation would you expect here?

2   What does the lack of punctuation suggest about the women's voices and the nature of their talk?

Many poems make use of a created **persona**. The use of a narrative 'I' might indicate the poet speaking directly to the reader, or an invented person. If you're studying Philip Larkin, for instance, it would be very tempting to think that the self-deprecating, rather melancholy voice in many of the poems is that of the poet – but is it always? On the other hand, it's perfectly clear that many of the voices created by U. A. Fanthorpe are not hers, as she 'speaks' as foxes, a fairy, and a cat, for example.

A created persona will often seek to show an understanding of the world seen from this person's angle, and to make the reader reflect on the speaker too. Here is the second stanza of Fanthorpe's 'The Invitation', where the voice is that of 'The Gloucestershire foxes':

> Us knows the pack be after thee,
> Us knows how that du end,
> The chase, the kill, the cheering,
> Dying wi'out a friend.

The dialect grammar and spelling here, and the sounds created by accent, are important parts of the voice, suggesting rural simplicity, but a simplicity which can speak directly to the child. The hunting, though, makes the reader think about the persecution of both participants, the foxes and Jesus. Further on in the poem, it is men who are referred to as 'beastly', a deliberately ambiguous word which makes the reader consider the nature of man.

ACTIVITY 69

Look at these openings of two poems by Carol Ann Duffy. 'Havisham' begins:

> Beloved sweetheart bastard.

'The Biographer' begins:

> Because you are dead,
> I stand at your desk, . . .

How are the speakers' characters established in these few words? Think about attitudes, relationship to other people, language.

Structure

In relatively short literary texts, like most of the poems you're likely to study in this module, openings and endings take on particular importance, in terms of the ways they shape meanings. In Activity 69 above, for instance, both openings are very direct and immediate, establishing a voice and an audience. The opening to Fanthorpe's 'The Wicked Fairy at the Manger' is similar: 'My gift for the child:', on an isolated line, followed by a line space, creates an immediate context and voice.

Because many modern poems isolate and reflect on a particular moment of experience, openings are often quite casual too, or even conversational, like 'Havisham'. Larkin's 'Whitsun Weddings' opens 'That Whitsun, I was late getting away', while 'Dockery and Son' begins with the snatch of conversation that sets the occasion for the whole poem:

'Dockery was junior to you,
Wasn't he?' said the Dean.

ACTIVITY 70

An 'immediate' opening is likely to be arresting for the reader. Look at the first two lines of Duffy's 'Oslo':

What you do. Follow the slow tram
into the night. Wear your coat with the hood.

What is unusual about these lines? Look at the grammar – the types of sentences here and the syntax. Remember that the reader has read the poem title, and made associations with it.

Poems often move from a specific moment, through reflection on the moment to a universal idea. This is true of several of Larkin's poems in the collection, *The Whitsun Weddings*. Working from the opening shown above on page 152, for instance, the last four lines of 'Dockery and Son' begin 'Life is first boredom, then fear'. Another poem 'Reference Back' shows this structure very clearly. The first line is:

That was a pretty one, I heard you call

The second stanza begins:

Oliver's *Riverside Blues*, it was. And now
I shall, I suppose, always remember how

The third and final stanza opens:

Truly, though our element is time,

'Truly' is one of the indicators here of the 'lesson' being drawn for the reader.

ACTIVITY 71

Read through this complete poem by Larkin, 'Home is so Sad'.

Home is so sad. It stays as it was left,
Shaped to the comfort of the last to go
As if to win them back. Instead, bereft
Of anyone to please, it withers so,
Having no heart to put aside the theft

And turn again to what it started as,
A joyous shot at how things ought to be,
Long fallen wide. You can see how it was:
Look at the pictures and the cutlery.
The music in the piano stool. That vase.

This is a variation on the structure shown in 'Reference Back'. Try to find the particular moment, the reflection on it, and then the 'universal' thought. How is this poem structured?

Endings, of course, often gather to a line or phrase which sums up the thought in the poem, or makes the reader reflect on what has gone before. In Duffy, for instance, 'the way everything dies' sums up the melancholy lessons of 'The Grammar of Light', while 'This will kill my folks' is a witty and poignant reflection on the story and the speaker in 'The Suicide'. '*Right*, said the baby. *That was roughly/What we had in mind*' is an apparently sudden shift at the end of Fanthorpe's 'The Wicked Fairy', which makes the reader consider the baby, the fairy, and the meaning of the Christmas story. Similarly, 'When thou tires of humanity' at the end of 'The Invitation' startles with the unusual word 'humanity' (unusual for the foxes), and jolts the reader into a reconsideration of meaning.

Time is often an element in shaping the structure of poems. In Larkin's 'Reference Back', for example, there are a number of time settings referred to: the time of writing, the time of the experience, and the recording of the music, and the poem moves around these. Duffy's 'Before You Were Mine', which opens: 'I'm ten years away from the corner you laugh on/With your pals', moves between her mother's youth, her own childhood, and the time of writing.

Language

Sentence lengths and **syntax** are language features which can be used to shape meanings. The effect of long and short sentences in Larkin's 'Here' has been looked at on page 152. Carol Ann Duffy often uses short phrases or even single words for effect, such as 'Ambition. Rage. Boredom. Spite' to capture the disaffection of the children she's been reading to in 'Like Earning a Living'.

ACTIVITY 72

In 'Fraud', Duffy's view of Robert Maxwell's character through his voice, she even splits words:

So read my lips. Mo-ney. Pow-er. Fame.

What effect do the breaks have, do you think? Consider why the tycoon might want to say these words slowly.

Syntax can be unusual, too. You could look at the verbless opening lines of Fanthorpe's 'The Room Where Everyone Goes', and at Duffy's 'Confession', with its lack of punctuation, to find the effects of these choices.

Paying attention to poets' uses of particular parts of speech can often reveal how meanings are being shaped. The use of the pronoun 'I' to create voice has already been mentioned, and the use of 'we' can create a sense of universality, as in 'all we do' and 'dulls to distance all we are' from Larkin's 'Ambulances'.

ACTIVITY 73

Read the last stanza of 'The Whitsun Weddings':

There we were aimed. And as we raced across
    Bright knots of rail
Past standing Pullmans, walls of blackened moss
Came close, and it was nearly done, this frail
Travelling coincidence; and what it held
Stood ready to be loosed with all the power
That being changed can give. We slowed again,
And as the tightened brakes took hold, there swelled
A sense of falling, like an arrow-shower
Sent out of sight, somewhere becoming rain.

'We' is simply referring to the people on the train. The interest here is in the verbs.

1 Begin by picking out all the verbs.

2 This poem begins with very slow movement; look back at Activity 67 above. How do the verbs suggest speed and power here? How else is speed suggested? (Look at the effect of the short line.)

3 As the train comes towards a halt with 'We slowed again', something new and different happens. What connection in sound is made between 'slowed' and a verb in the next line? Where does the 'sense of falling' come from, do you think?

4 The first verb is 'aimed'. How does this both match the direction of the train, and prepare the reader for the end of the poem?

Poets are fond of using unusual or even invented words for effect.
U. A. Fanthorpe, for instance, uses the word 'widdershins', an archaic word meaning left-handed, or in a strange way, in 'The Silence' to suggest the ancient writers of the words on the slate. Similarly, Duffy uses the archaic word 'trow,' meaning think, or believe, in 'Beachcomber' to capture the narrator's effort to go back in memory to an earlier time.

Words can be used to suggest things, by playing on ideas and associations. The last line of Fanthorpe's 'The Room Where Everyone Goes' is:

The scent of the commonplace brings them home.

'Scent', ironically refers to the smell of the toilet, and 'the commonplace' is ambiguous – it means both 'the ordinary' and the common place, i.e. the place which is common to everybody, in any time period, and in any 'home'. Here it could mean 'brings the past back to life', perhaps.

ACTIVITY 74

In 'Sirensong' Fanthorpe describes the sound of enemy bombers above the house in the war:

The house fluttered,
As trespassing aircraft droned life-long overhead,

What do you think 'life-long' might mean or imply here? Think about time, the listener's perception of time, and what might happen. The moment is described by an older person looking back, too, which might suggest a further meaning.

The word 'fluttered' is a **personification**. What might the poet be suggesting by using the word 'fluttered'? Think about the house and its occupants.

Playing with words also means playing with the readers' expectations as language unfolds. At the beginning of 'Queening It', Fanthorpe writes:

Inside every man there lurks the Widow Twankey,
Brazen and bosomed as a figurehead,
Dressed to the tens, . . .

The opening five words suggest something quite serious or heroic, so that 'The Widow Twankey' comes as a shock, and a ludicrous one. 'As a figurehead' suggests something monumental, overpainted and sticking out at the front. 'Dressed to the tens' continues the 'over the top' idea, but 'tens' still comes as a surprise; Fanthorpe uses and changes the cliché of 'dressed to the nines' to humorous effect.

Carol Ann Duffy revels in playing and experimenting with words. 'Go on. G'on. Gon' at the end of 'Away and See' sounds like an auctioneer's closing words, with the missing final 'e' suggesting the subject has already departed. Donna who 'dunno' in 'Like Earning a Living' is one of many puns in her poems.

ACTIVITY 75

The speaker in Duffy's 'The Cliché Kid' speaks in clichés. Here's the last stanza:

Sweet Jesus, Doc, I worry I'll miss when a long time dead
the smell the smell the smell of the baby's head,
the fresh-baked grass, dammit, the new mown bread . . .

1 How many clichés can you find here?

2 Why is 'the smell' repeated three times, do you think?

3 The kid is confused. How does Duffy show this in the last line by changing the expected words?

Irony depends on word play and association. A clear example is the title of Fanthorpe's 'Christmas Presents'. The 'present' is not gold, but the presentation of a future beyond the present; but more grimly, Christmas presents, or brings, death to the inhabitant of the bed next to the narrator's.

The sound of words are a vital ingredient of poetry; many poems are written to be read aloud, and even if they're not, or you're not in a situation where they can be read aloud, you should hear them in your head. You couldn't understand what Duffy means by the apparently invented word 'Kin-L' in 'Like Earning a Living' without saying or hearing it aloud, for instance, and you might not notice that in 'Fraud' she ends every line with the letter 'm', perhaps to imply a connection with the huge ego of the man who was 'Private M'.

ACTIVITY 76

Read the end of Duffy's poem 'Havisham'.

Bang. I stabbed at a wedding-cake.
Give me a male corpse for a long slow honeymoon.
Don't think it's only the heart that b-b-b-breaks.

1 Which sound is repeated in the first line? Why this short, sharp sound?

2 Look at the vowel sounds at the end of the second line. How do they match what is being described?

3 Finally, what do you make of the sound created by 'b-b-b-breaks'? Havisham has been bitter throughout the poem. What change might the writer be suggesting here through the sound of this word?

Repetition and listing are often employed, too, as in the repetition of 'the smell' in Activity 75 above. Here's an extract from Philip Larkin's 'Here':

And residents from raw estates, brought down
The dead straight miles by stealing flat-faced trolleys,
Push through plate-glass swing doors to their desires –
Cheap suits, red kitchen-ware, sharp shoes, iced lollies,
Electric mixers, toasters, washers, driers –

The list of goods reflects both the desires of the buyers, and therefore their nature, and the attitude of the poet to them. The list is prepared for by the estates being described as 'raw', and the trolleys as 'stealing' and 'flat-faced'. The words suggest cheapness, hardness and unattractive poverty, and this is reflected in the list. The first word is 'cheap', the colour garish, the shoes suggest flashiness rather than style, and the list of four items in the fourth line suggests greed and materialism in itself, as no particular attributes are mentioned for any of the items.

ACTIVITY 77

Look at another list, this time from Larkin's poem 'The Large Cool Store':

But past the heaps of shirts and trousers
Spread the stands of Modes For Night:
Machine-embroidered, thin as blouses,

Lemon, sapphire, moss-green, rose,
Bri-Nylon Baby-Dolls and Shorties
Flounce in clusters . . . .

Later on in the poem Larkin suggests that both love and women can seem to be 'synthetic' and 'natureless'. How does this list help to shape his meaning? Think about the effect of the capital letters in 'Modes For Night', the mention of manufacture and materials, the colours, and the effect of 'Flounce'.

Duffy and Fanthorpe are both poets who are very conscious of how language works, and use this sense overtly. In 'Moments of Grace', Duffy compares people to parts of speech, and to poems, and in 'Adultery' she ends:

> and all for the same thing twice. And all
> for the same thing twice. You did it.
> What. Didn't you. Fuck. Fuck. No. That was
> the wrong verb. This is only an abstract noun.

The repetitions are interesting here. The repeated sentence has a sense of emptiness and defeat in 'all for'. 'The same thing twice' may suggest the second liaison, not simply a repeated sexual act, and the line break after 'all' the second time emphasises the emptiness, while repeating 'the same thing twice' draws attention to the device of repetition deliberately. The deliberately crude 'fuck', with its hard, short, repeated sound, not only echoes the act, but becomes a curse, perhaps. The verb is 'wrong', perhaps suggesting something wrong about the act, as well as the wrong word to use, and the noun being 'abstract' – presumably referring the reader back to the title – suggests something not, in the end, real.

ACTIVITY 78

Here's an example of U. A. Fanthorpe playing with the language of literature in 'Painter and Poet'. She compares the two artists:

> Having only
> Himself to please, he tinkers at pleasing himself.
> Watch silently now as that metaphor
> Fans slowly out, like a fin from the sea.
> Did you notice him then, secret and shy as an otter,
> Transferring an epithet? See that artless adverb
> Mature into a pun!

1 How does the poet play with words in the first sentence?

2 Look at the phrase the 'metaphor fans'. What part of speech is the word 'fans', in fact?

3 The echo of fans/fins makes a connection. But what sort of figure of speech is 'like a fin from the sea'?

4 How is the idea of something coming from the sea continued, and in what figure of speech?

The play on words introduces the idea of 'a pun', although Fanthorpe doesn't give the reader one, just when it's expected.

Poets employ various kinds of **imagery** – drawing pictures which help the reader to understand the thought or feeling being expressed – to shape meanings, in other words.

In Activity 73 you looked at the end of 'The Whitsun Weddings', where Larkin describes the sense of falling as being 'like an arrow-shower/Sent out of sight, somewhere becoming rain.' There are two images here: the **simile** 'like an arrow-shower' suggests speed, as though the speed of the train has continued to drive them; a certain, fast movement towards an uncertain end ('out of sight'); and a continuation of what the train brought together, which is prepared for by the word 'aimed' at the beginning of the last stanza. 'Becoming rain' is a **metaphor**, developing from the visual image of the arrow-shower. 'Rain' is appropriate for something falling from the sky, the picture that the arrow-shower has evoked, and it could suggest a melancholy outcome, which the reader could see as typical of some of Larkin's poetry. On the other hand, rain falling also suggests fertility, appropriate for the newly married couples, and this possibility is prepared for with the description of London's 'postal districts packed like squares of wheat' – another image, which interestingly depends on a view from above, an arrow or rain's eye view.

ACTIVITY 79

Read this extract from Larkin's 'Love Songs in Age':

> . . . the unfailing sense of being young
> Spread out like a spring-woken tree, wherein
>   That hidden freshness, sung,
> That certainty of time laid up in store
> As when she played them first. But, even more,
>
> The glare of that much-mentioned brilliance, love,
>   Broke out, to show
> Its bright incipience sailing above,
> Still promising to solve, and satisfy,
> And set unchangeably in order . . .

1 How is the sense of being young like a tree conveyed? Think about both 'spring-woken' and 'spread'.

2 Where is 'that hidden freshness', exactly?

3 What is love being compared to at the beginning of the second stanza? How do you know? (there are several indications)

4 Love is personified too, in the last two lines. How?

At the end of Fanthorpe's 'Dying Fall', the poet refuses to celebrate war.

> Skulls, tongueless bells, miming their message,
> Waiting for the wind to say.

Skulls are like bells in shape, and both have tongues, which gives the poet the opportunity to shape the end of the poem. These skulls have no tongues, suggesting decomposition, perhaps, so their message has to be 'mimed' – they speak wordlessly; it is their appearance which conveys the message. Grimly, the wind will 'say' – a personification, suggesting that the message lies in the leaves blown into the gutter, and the mud. Death, in other words.

ACTIVITY 80

Fanthorpe's 'Atlas' is about the strength of a particular kind of love. Read the last stanza:

And maintenance is the sensible side of love,
Which knows what time and weather are doing
To my brickwork; insulates my faulty wiring;
Laughs at my dryrotten jokes; remembers
My need for gloss and grouting; which keeps
My suspect edifice upright in air,
As Atlas did the sky.

The whole stanza is built on the comparison between the speaker and a house.

1   Work out all the comparisons, and what the speaker's partner is actually doing, then reflect on how this 'maintenance' is 'the sensible side of love'.

2   The comparison in the last line is different, though: Atlas wasn't a builder, after all. What does this comparison tell you about the partner, and the speaker's attitude to the partner?

In 'Adultery' Carol Ann Duffy writes these lines about remembering an adulterous encounter:

. . . a slow replay in the kitchen
where the slicing of innocent onions
scalds you to tears. Then, selfish autobiographical sleep

in a marital bed, the tarnished spoon of your body
stirring betrayal, your heart over-ripe at the core.

The 'slow replay' likens the memory to a filmic record. The slicing of onions would produce tears naturally, but Duffy plays with this idea by attaching the word 'innocent' to the onions. The onions are 'innocent' of the knowledge, of course, but there are other possibilities: the speaker could be thinking about the destruction of her own innocence, or the damage to her marital partner, who is also 'innocent' of the knowledge. The tears are produced by the slicing which 'scalds', suggesting the heat of tears, but also damage unlike the usual response to onions. The stirring of the body in bed prompts the idea of it being like a spoon, but stirring betrayal instead of sugar; after all, the stirring of the body in another bed is the betrayal. The spoon is 'tarnished', suggesting the speaker's guilt. The heart is like a fruit, 'over-ripe at the core', suggesting that out of sight, but also in the centre, the heart is too full: there are two people in there. 'Over-ripe' is not a healthy state, either; it's too rich, too far gone – excessive.

ACTIVITY 81

Here is a stanza from Duffy's 'Stafford Afternoons':

I knew it was dangerous. The way the trees
drew sly faces from light and shade, the wood
let out its sticky breath on the back of my neck,
and flowering nettles gathered spit in their throats.

The child has put herself in a dangerous situation. There are three personifications here – things which aren't human are given human characteristics. Pick these out, and decide how each of them suggests a threat to the child.

> AO4: articulate independent opinions and judgements informed by different interpretations of literary texts by other readers

This is the dominant Assessment Objective on the twentieth-century texts on this paper, carrying 10 of the 20 marks available. The questions are likely to give a view of the text and the writer, and ask for your opinion. Before considering how you might form a response, it's worth thinking about what the subjects of the questions might be. Broadly, they could focus on the poet's concerns, and how the poet conveys them; the poet's techniques; or the qualities of the poet's work. As an example, here's a list of some of the things which could form the focus of questions about Larkin, Fanthorpe and Duffy. This is not an exhaustive list, by any means, just some examples.

Larkin

- experience bringing disillusionment/loss/uncertainty/regret

- the approach of death

- time

- the hopelessness of love

- how Larkin conveys joy

- how Larkin conveys place

- conversational tone

- moving from specific experiences to universal thoughts

Fanthorpe

- giving voices to those without voices
- using the past to reflect on the present
- war
- the meaning of Christmas
- wit/word play
- love
- houses
- first-person poems: the creation of personae

Duffy

- schooldays
- family relationships
- loss of innocence
- poems focusing on particular characters
- autobiographical poems
- love
- the effects of time/shifting perspective
- the past
- use of language/word play
- creation of personae
- loss and betrayal

Forming a response

As an example, let's suppose that you were studying Larkin, and that the question you were going to tackle was:

'A critic considered that Larkin was only interested in the exploration of despair. Do you agree with this view?'

You know that:

- you have to consider the critic's view

- you have to write about form, structure and language, not just meanings – the word 'exploration' suggests it anyway

- you must reach an 'independent opinion'.

First of all, what material would you use? To consider how the critic has come to this view, you might want to think about poems like 'Mr Bleaney', 'Love Songs in Age', 'Home is so Sad', 'Days', 'Talking in Bed', 'As Bad as a Mile', 'Ambulances', 'Dockery and Son' and 'Reference Back', and choose ones where you can consider technique as well as ideas. The last two poems, for instance, are both structured towards a universal view of loss and death. 'As Bad as a Mile' uses the biting of the apple as a symbol of failure. 'Dockery and Son', too, uses striking imagery of closure and uncertainty, and manipulates form to suggest exclusion (see Activity 66).

You might then think about an opposing view, using the positive moods in 'For Sidney Bechet', 'First Sight' and 'An Arundel Tomb', perhaps. You need to cite examples of technique as well, though, such as the exclamations in 'For Sidney Bechet', the use of lambs as symbols in 'First Sight', and the effect of the last line in 'An Arundel Tomb'.

With some material in mind, you would then go about structuring a response, keeping the critic's view firmly in mind. You should look to develop and qualify your arguments, too; here, for instance, you could take into account that the music in 'For Sidney Bechet' creates 'appropriate falsehood' and scatters 'long-haired grief and scored pity'; that the 'immeasurable surprise' in 'First Sight' which the lambs will meet will not necessarily be pleasant; and that the apparently affirmative last line of 'An Arundel Tomb' is undermined by the previous line. To conclude, your personal view must be evident, and it must be clear that you have reached the judgement *informed by different interpretations of literary texts by other readers*.

Summary

This concludes the section on Pre 1900 and Post 1900 poetry. You have seen how contexts and the writers' ways of expressing ideas related to these contexts are logically linked and you have become aware of the great variety of contexts. You have had some practice in evaluating both the ideas behind the literature and the ways in which the writers' choices of form, structure and language shape meanings.

So you now have the necessary 'knowledge and understanding' to help you prepare for your examination in this module, which is 'open book'.

Approaching the Examinations

Revision

As the examinations for your modules get closer, you will need to think about revision, and how you can set about it in a focused way. There are two important elements you need to think about: acquiring knowledge, and thinking about the Assessment Objectives for the questions on the paper.

Knowledge

Whatever you write in the exams on set texts, you'll need to demonstrate your knowledge by supporting your views with quotations from the text, echoes of the texts, details of the text. There are no short cuts here, and no substitute for re-reading the text several times. After all, at each reading you don't simply remember more of it, you also add to your store of understanding, as more and more of the way the text works is revealed to you. It's impossible to understand a text fully from one reading. It would be nice to think that you could, but you can't.

If you read your texts often enough, there'll be no problem in providing good support for what you want to say about the text in response to the exam question. There's no point in 'learning the best 15 quotations to use' – you don't know what the 'best' material is until you see the question. The evidence you should use is *appropriate* evidence.

The examination for Module 1 could well be the first time you've taken a closed book exam in English Literature, and you might find this worrying – but you shouldn't. Having the text with you is only to allow 'open book' style questions – ones which ask you to re-examine carefully a section of the text or to use a given extract as a starting point for discussion. Its purpose isn't to provide knowledge after all, you can't start reading the book in the exam and you won't have the time to start looking things up. Looked at this way, there's no real difference between open and closed book exams.

Assessment Objectives

The focus of this whole book has been on the Assessment Objectives for your course in English Literature, and now isn't the time to forget about them. Your revision should revolve around a consideration of the Assessment Objectives you'll be tested on for each text, so you need to look for and explore these within the text. Of course, this means revisiting the work you've done in and outside class, but it's also where the focus of your re-readings should be.

To help you revise the Assessment Objectives, here's an exercise on them, and how they are used to read a text. Below is an extract from the play *The Steamie* by Tony Roper. 'Steamies' were communal laundries in Glasgow.

MAGRIT   . . . Apart fae you dae mean?

ANDY   Cause. [*Glasgow drunk's hand-signals.*] Zat what ah'm here for . . . now then . . . Z'ivrything awright?

MAGRIT   [*this speech should be done with heavy irony to the audience as she sings 'Isn't it wonderful to be a woman'*] Isn't it wonderful tae be a woman. Ye get up at the crack o' dawn and get the breakfast oan, get the weans ready and oot the hoose lookin' as tidy and as well dressed as ye can afford. Then ye see tae the lord high provider and get him oot, then wash up, finish the ironin', tidy the hoose and gie the flair a skite o'er. Then it's oot tae yer ain wee job, mebbe cleanin' offices, servin' in a shop or washin' stairs. Then it's dinner time. Well it is fur everybody else but no us 'cause we don't get dinner. By the time yer oot and run home, cooked something for the weans, yer lucky if you feel like something tae eat. I know I don't and even if I did . . . the dinner hour's finished, so it's back tae yer work; that is efter ye've goat in whatever yer gonnae gie them for their tea, and efter yer finished yer work, ye'r back up . . . cookin' again and they'll tell ye the mince is lumpy . . . or the chips are too warm . . . then they're away oot. The weans tae play . . . the men tae have a drink, cause they need wan . . . the souls . . . efter pittin' in a hard day's graft, so ye've goat the hoose tae yersel' and what dae ye dae, ye tidy up again don't ye? Mer ironin, light the fire, wash the dishes and the pots etc. etc. and then ye sit doon. And what happens . . . ye've just sat doon when the weans come up. 'Gonnae make us a cuppa tea and something tae eat' . . . What dae ye's want tae eat? . . . 'Och anything Ma' . . . D'ye want some o' that soup? . . . 'Naw' . . . A tomato sandwich? . . . 'Naw' . . . A couple o' boiled eggs? . . . 'Naw' . . . A piece 'n spam? . . . 'Naw' . . . Well what d'ye's want? . . . 'Och anything at all'. So ye make them something tae eat then ye sit doon and finally have a wee blaw . . . a very wee blaw . . . cause it's time tae go tae the steamie. Ye go tae the steamie, finish at nine o'clock and get the washin' hame. Ye sort it aw oot . . . and get it put by and then sometimes mebbe take stock of yer life. What are we? . . . skivvies . . . unpaid skivvies . . . in other words we are . . . used . . . but ye think tae yersel', well even if I am being used . . . I don't mind . . . cause I love my family and anyway it's New Year's Eve. I can relax and jist enjoy masel . . . and any minute noo the weans'll be in an ma friends'll be comin' roon wi' black bun, shortbread, dumplin's, a wee refreshment and I can forget aw ma worries even if it's jist for a night and the weans arrive and ye gie them shortbread, sultana cake, ginger wine and there is just one thing missin', the

> head of the family. The door bell goes, ye open the door, and what is staunin there, ready to make the evening complete . . . that's right . . . your husband, your better half . . . the man who was goin' to make you the happiest woman in the world and [*Gently.*] what does he look like . . . *that* [At ANDY.]
>
> DOLLY   Who were ye talkin' tae?
>
> MAGRIT   Masel.
>
> ANDY   So . . . z'a . . . wis sayin' girls . . . everything aw right doon here . . . know . . . cause . . . that's what I'm here fur.

What can you find in the passage which relates to Assessment Objectives 2i–5i? Remember that you need to provide evidence from the text for all your ideas. Here are some of the things you might think about:

AO2i: This is obviously from a play, but 'type' means more than genre. What type of play do you think it might be? What is the period? Think about the period that the play is set in, and the period when it was written – they might not be the same.

AO3: *Form* What is the effect of the stage directions? Who do you think Magrit's words are spoken to? This might make you speculate about the form of the whole play.

Language The language is obviously dialect, and the information given tells you it's Glasgow dialect. But there's a lot more to see. Think about the effect of the pronouns. Think about how humour is created, particularly with rhythm and repetition. Think about the tone – which words are obviously ironic? There's more, of course.

Structure Looking at the pronouns in the extract, and thinking about the form of the play, might make you think about the structure, both of the passage here, and of the whole play. Look at the shape of Magrit's speech. How is it structured to finish the way it does?

AO4: Two obvious readings of the text are Marxist and feminist. Look for evidence of both. Is this really a feminist piece? Look carefully at the end of Magrit's speech.

AO5i: What different contexts can you find? Think about cultural, social and historical contexts, and the context of literary type and period.

In the examination

The most important thing to remember in the examination room is the importance of thinking and planning. You're full of knowledge, we hope, but it's easy to misuse it in the pressure of the exam, or at least not to use it effectively. Here's what you should do:

- Deconstruct the question. You know which Assessment Objectives are being targeted: look carefully for how they appear in the question, and at exactly what you're being asked to do. There's time allowed for thinking in the exam room. You've spent a long time reading your text, so you can afford the time to read the question several times, to make sure where the thrust of your response should be. There is a particular danger when you think you 'recognise' a question. You probably don't; it just looks a bit like something you've thought about, and it's all too easy to set off happily on the wrong track.

- Plan your response in detail. Structuring responses carefully, in a logical progression, will enable you to communicate your views clearly. Don't skip this; all too often candidates produce unstructured responses in the exam, in which the answer to the question doesn't start until halfway through.

- If you've planned clearly, you can spend your writing time following your plan, and choosing the best words and the best evidence to support what you say as you go.

Remember that in Module 3 you have to answer two questions, and you should aim to split your time equally between the two.

Glossary

Allegory an extended metaphor, usually a narrative or description which works on two levels simultaneously. It usually carries a hidden moral meaning; for example, George Orwell's *Animal Farm*.

Alliteration a sequence of two or more words beginning with the same letter placed close together, for example: 'Full fathom five thy father lies'.

Ambiguity occurs when it is possible to draw two or more meanings out of a literary work; for example, it is possible to read *Dr Faustus* as a warning about pride, or as a query about whether mankind may have such moral certainties as sin and redemption.

Archaic the use of a word, phrase or style which is deliberately old-fashioned and no longer in popular use; for example, the use of the word 'glebe' in Gray's 'Elegy written in a Country Churchyard'.

Association is the range of meanings which a word has acquired which have a personal significance to the user. *See* connotation.

Assonance the similarity of vowel sounds without actual rhyme, for example: 'May reap his conquest, and may least rejoice?' Here Milton repeats the 'ee' sound to make contrasts in the line.

Chivalric code the rule of behaviour for knights in medieval times as defined in *The Romance of the Rose*, and evident as subject-matter in Chaucer's writing.

Colloquialism informal language with familiar modes of speech as opposed to a formal use of language.

Conceit a far-fetched comparison in which you are forced to admit likeness between two things, whilst always being aware of the oddness of the comparison. The Metaphysical poets were famed for their use of conceits, such as Donne's image of the compasses to describe two lovers.

Connotation the extended significances of a word which are generally agreed; for example, purple is generally linked to royalty, mourning or Lent. *See* association.

Context in AS Literary Studies this is the new fifth Assessment Objective. Contexts are the important facts, events or processes which have helped to shape literary works, for example, characteristics of contemporary styles.

Courtly love the code of behaviour a knight must follow in courting his lady in medieval times. This was defined in *The Romance of the Rose*, and forms part of Chaucer's subject-matter.

Demotic popular, colloquial or vulgar language.

Detachment used when a writer adopts an impartial view of things.

Dialect is a form of language which is specific to a region or district, in which there is a particular idiom, pronunciation or vocabulary. For example, 'Scouse' is the Liverpudlian dialect.

Dialogue the part of literary works, particularly plays, written as conversation.

Diction is the vocabulary, the set of words a writer uses, for example, learned, homely, colloquial, archaic, etc.

Digression a part of a literary work in which the writer appears to have drifted away from the main subject.

Double entendre a phrase with two meanings, one of which is usually indecent, for example Wycherley's use of 'china' in *The Country Wife*.

Dramatic irony a situation in drama where the audience knows more than the characters on stage.

Dramatic monologue a first-person narrative account in verse or prose.

End-stopped rhyme rhyming lines which contain a complete thought in each line.

Epilogue the concluding part of a literary work in which originally the actors addressed the audience; an author may address an epilogue at the end of a work to the reader, for example, Jane Austen's address to the reader at the end of *Mansfield Park*.

Figurative language language which contains figures of speech, for example, similes or metaphors.

Genre a specific type or style of literature or art.

Half-rhyme a type of verse in which the rhyme is not full, for example, rhyme created by assonance. *See* assonance.

Heroic couplet iambic pentameters rhyming in pairs, originally used by Pope and Dryden, but also used by writers such as Chaucer and Keats. *See* iambic pentameter.

Iambic pentameter a line of poetry with five weakly stressed syllables each followed by five strongly stressed syllables, for example Shakespeare's:

ᵕ ╱ ᵕ ╱ ᵕ ╱ ᵕ ╱ ᵕ ╱
When I do count the clock that tells the time.

Imagery images used by a writer of poetry or prose in which a picture or sense-impression is conveyed in words.

Impressionistic a style of writing in which impressions are conveyed by a non-realistic account of successive details, for example, the writing of Virginia Woolf and James Joyce.

Interior monologue used when a writer conveys to the reader the thoughts of a character as they are being experienced.

Interlacing part of the medieval principle of construction in which ideas are woven together intricately.

Internal rhyme a line in poetry where there is rhyming inside the line.

Irony present in writing of speech when the real meaning is concealed in words suggesting the opposite meaning, often as a means of criticism; for example, in the works of Jane Austen, Thomas Hardy and Jonathan Swift.

Metaphor an implied or compressed comparison when one thing is said to take on the qualities of another, for example, Shakespeare's 'There's daggers in men's smiles'.

Metaphysical a literary term invented by Dryden to describe a group of seventeenth-century poets characterised by the use of far-fetched imagery and witty conceits. *See* conceit.

Metre the arrangement of stressed and unstressed syllables in a line of verse to produce a certain effect.

Miltonic literary writing in the style of Milton; when used about the sonnet form this indicates a sonnet composed of an octet followed by a sestet. *See* Petrarchan, octet and sestet.

Morality play medieval drama in verse in which abstractions such as Vice and Virtue were presented on stage, for example, *Everyman*.

Motif a dominant idea or image which reappears throughout a work, such as the use of the colour red in *The Handmaid's Tale*.

Objective the presentation of ideas uninfluenced by the writer's feelings or opinions.

Octet in the sonnet form the first eight-line section of a Miltonic sonnet.

Parody the use of another writer's form and style, sometimes to create satirical or comic effect.

Persona the adapting by a writer of the personality of someone else.

Personification the reference to an abstract idea in prose or poetry, as though it were a person, for example, Donne's address to death in his 'Divine Sonnet'.

Petrarchan the sonnet form originally created by Petrarch in the fourteenth century, and later used by Milton amongst others. *See* Miltonic.

Quatrain a stanza or sequence of four lines, sometimes with alternate rhymes.

Register a set of words used in specific circumstances or time period, for example, in writing about war a military register might be used by Wilfred Owen.

Satire literary work in which the aim is to amuse, criticise or correct by means of ridicule, for example, the works of Jane Austen.

Sensual related to the senses or sensations, usually with a sexual connotation rather than spiritual or intellectual.

Sensuous appealing to the senses but with no restriction to fleshly or sexual pleasure.

Sestet the second part of a Miltonic sonnet consisting of six lines.

Shakespearean sonnet the sonnet form used by Shakespeare, consisting of three quatrains and a final summative couplet, or two rhymed lines.

Sibilance a series of words with a hissing sound such as 's' and 'sh'.

Simile a figure of speech using 'as' or 'like' in which there is a comparison used for clarity or vividness, for example, Coleridge's 'as idle as a painted ship'.

Stanza another name for a verse in a poem, with a set number of rhymes. The word comes from the Italian 'little room', as successive stanzas in a poem were seen to be like the rooms in a house, separate, but each leading out of one another.

Stream of consciousness a literary style which follows, without obvious external structuring, the internal successive thought processes of a character, such as in the writings of Virginia Woolf and James Joyce.

Subjective writing which aims to promote a personal point of view, and which is therefore not impartial.

Surrealism writing in which things are presented as though perceived in a dream or in the subconscious mind, and not in a way which would seem to be realistic in an everyday way.

Symbolism a literary style originated in France in the nineteenth century in which the writer tries to create impressions rather than to describe things accurately.

Syntax the grammatical arrangement of words in writing or speech.

Theology the science or study of religion concerned with the knowledge of God.